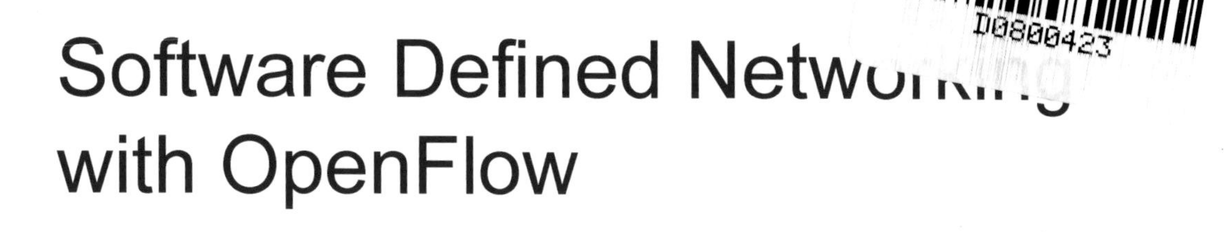

Software Defined Networking with OpenFlow

Get hands-on with the platforms and development tools used to build OpenFlow network applications

Siamak Azodolmolky

BIRMINGHAM - MUMBAI

Software Defined Networking with OpenFlow

First published: October 2013

Production Reference: 1211013

Published by Packt Publishing Ltd.
Livery Place
35 Livery Street
Birmingham B3 2PB, UK.

ISBN 978-1-84969-872-6

www.packtpub.com

Cover Image by Mrunal Gawade (mrunal.gawade@gmail.com)

Credits

Author
Siamak Azodolmolky

Reviewers
Prof. Dr. Christian Esteve Rothenberg
Seungwon Shin

Acquisition Editor
Julian Ursell

Commissioning Editor
Manasi Pandire

Technical Editors
Manan Badani
Nadeem Bagban
Tanvi Bhatt
Pankaj Kadam
Pramod Kumavat
Sonali Vernekar

Project Coordinator
Akash Poojary

Proofreader
Faye Coulman
Linda Morris

Indexer
Hemangini Bari

Graphics
Ronak Dhruv
Abhinash Sahu

Production Coordinator
Melwyn D'sa

Cover Work
Melwyn D'sa

About the Author

Siamak Azodolmolky received his Computer Engineering degree from Tehran University and his first MSc. degree in Computer Architecture from Azad University in 1994 and 1998 respectively. He was employed by Data Processing Iran Co. (IBM in Iran) as a Software Developer, Systems Engineer, and as a Senior R&D Engineer during 1992-2001. He received his second MSc. degree with distinction from Carnegie Mellon University in 2006. He joined Athens Information Technology (AIT) as a Research Scientist and Software Developer in 2007, while pursuing his PhD degree. In August 2010, he joined the High Performance Networks research group of the School of Computer Science and Electronic Engineering (CSEE) of the University of Essex as a Senior Research Officer. He received his PhD (with 'cum laude') from the Universitat Politécnica de Catalunya UPC in 2011. He has been the technical investigator of various national and EU funded projects. Software Defined Networking (SDN) has been one of his research interests since 2010, in which he has been investigating the extension of OpenFlow towards its application in core transport (optical) networks. He has published more than 50 scientific papers in international conferences, journals, and books. Currently, he is with Gesellschaft für Wissenschaftliche Datenverarbeitung mbH Göttingen (GWDG) as a Senior Researcher and has lead SDN related activities since September 2012. He is a professional member of ACM and a senior member of IEEE.

Whenever I reach the end of a book production, once again I realize that nobody is perfect. I would like to thank the technical reviewers for providing me with fruitful and constructive feedback. Any remaining errors are, of course, my own. I would also like to thank the Packt Publishing team who has been really supportive in getting this book off the ground. The knowledge, support, and experience of many colleagues in the SDN community have been instrumental in filling the gaps in my understanding of SDN. This book was not simply possible without them.

Finally, sincere and especially heartfelt thanks go out to my son, **Parsa Azodolmolky**. His patience during writing time, while being away from me is greatly appreciated. I love you Parsa.

About the Reviewers

Christian Esteve Rothenberg, has been an Assistant Professor at the University of Campinas (UNICAMP) since August 2013, where he received his PhD in Electrical and Computer Engineering in 2010. From 2010 to 2013, he worked as a Senior Research Scientist in the areas of IP systems and networking at CPqD R&D Center in Telecommunications, Campinas, Brazil. Christian was the technical lead of OpenFlow/SDN activities that resulted in RouteFlow and the first open source OpenFlow 1.2 and 1.3 software toolkits.

He holds a Telecommunication Engineering degree from the Technical University of Madrid (ETSIT-UPM), Spain, and an M.Sc. (Dipl. Ing.) degree in Electrical Engineering and Information Technology from the Darmstadt University of Technology (TUD), Germany in 2006. Christian holds two international patents and has published in scientific journals and top-tier networking conferences, such as SIGCOMM and INFOCOM. Since April 2013, Christian has been working as a Research Associate of the Open Networking Foundation (ONF).

Seungwon Shin has recently graduated in Computer Engineering from the Texas A&M University. His research topic was Software Defined Networking (SDN) Security. He has published more than 15 papers in academia and developed open source SDN security tools, FRESCO and FortNOX (and also, SE-FloodLight). Currently, he is working at Atto-Research, Korea, a startup company developing robust and secure OpenFlow controllers.

www.PacktPub.com

Support files, eBooks, discount offers and more

You might want to visit www.PacktPub.com for support files and downloads related to your book.

Did you know that Packt offers eBook versions of every book published, with PDF and ePub files available? You can upgrade to the eBook version at www.PacktPub.com and as a print book customer, you are entitled to a discount on the eBook copy. Get in touch with us at service@packtpub.com for more details.

At www.PacktPub.com, you can also read a collection of free technical articles, sign up for a range of free newsletters and receive exclusive discounts and offers on Packt books and eBooks.

http://PacktLib.PacktPub.com

Do you need instant solutions to your IT questions? PacktLib is Packt's online digital book library. Here, you can access, read and search across Packt's entire library of books.

Why Subscribe?

- Fully searchable across every book published by Packt
- Copy and paste, print and bookmark content
- On demand and accessible via web browser

Free Access for Packt account holders

If you have an account with Packt at www.PacktPub.com, you can use this to access PacktLib today and view nine entirely free books. Simply use your login credentials for immediate access.

Table of Contents

Preface

Decoupling the network control out of the networking devices is the common denominator of Software Defined Networking (SDN). SDN is a recent paradigm shift in computer networking, where network control functionality (also known as control plane) is decoupled from data forwarding functionality (also known as data plane) and furthermore the split control is programmable. The migration of control logic, which used to be tightly integrated in networking devices (for example, Ethernet switches) into accessible and logically centralized controllers, enables the underlying networking infrastructure to be abstracted from an applications point of view. This separation paves the way for a more flexible, programmable, vendor-agnostic, cost effective, and innovative network architecture. Besides the network abstraction, SDN architecture will provide a set of Application Programing Interfaces (APIs) that simplifies the implementation of common network services (for example, routing, multicast, security, access control, bandwidth management, traffic engineering, QoS, energy efficiency, and various forms of policy management). As a result, enterprises, network operators, and carriers gain unprecedented programmability, automation, and network control, enabling them to build highly scalable, flexible networks that readily adapt to changing business needs. OpenFlow is the first standard interface designed specifically for SDN, providing high performance, granular traffic control across multiple networking devices. This book looks at the fundamentals of OpenFlow, as one of the early implementations of the SDN concept. Starting from OpenFlow switches and controllers up to the development of OpenFlow-based network applications (Net Apps), network virtualization, OpenFlow in Cloud Computing, and a summary of active OpenFlow related open source projects are topics, which are covered in this book. If you are still hungry for more, this book shows you how to do SDN with OpenFlow.

What this book covers

Chapter 1, Introducing OpenFlow, introduces the OpenFlow and its role in the SDN ecosystem and how it works in a computer network. This chapter shapes the required knowledge prior to the actual setup of an experimental environment. The notion of flow, flow forwarding, OpenFlow functions, what can OpenFlow tables do, and features and limitations of OpenFlow are covered in this chapter.

Chapter 2, Implementing the OpenFlow Switch, covers the available implementations of OpenFlow switches including hardware and software implementations.

Chapter 3, The *OpenFlow Controllers*, covers the role of OpenFlow controllers as a control entity for OpenFlow switches and the provided API (that is, northbound interface) for the development of OpenFlow-based Network Applications (Net Apps).

Chapter4, Setting Up the Environment, introduces the options for OpenFlow switches and controllers. It also covers the environment for Net App development. This chapter focuses on the installation of virtual machines (VMs) and tools (for example, Mininet and Wireshark), which will be used in the next chapters for Net App development.

Chapter 5, "Net App" Development, covers developing of sample network applications (for example, learning switch and firewall) to show how OpenFlow provides the common ground for network application (Net App) development.

Chapter 6, Getting a Network Slice, covers the network slicing using OpenFlow and FlowVisor. A setup will be planned and the reader can understand how to configure and use a slice of the network using FlowVisor.

Chapter 7, OpenFlow in Cloud Computing, focuses on the role of OpenFlow in cloud computing and in particular, the installation and configuration of OpenStack's Neutron will be covered. Neutron is an incubated OpenStack project that provides network connectivity as a service (NaaS) between interface devices (for example, vNICs or virtual network interface cards), which are managed by other OpenStack services.

Chapter 8, Open Source Resources, explains and gives pointers to the important open source projects that network engineers and/or administrators can utilize in their production environment. These projects range from OpenFlow soft switches, Controllers, virtualization tools, Orchestration tools, to simulation and testing utilities.

What you need for this book

This book assumes that you have some level of network experience and knowledge such as TCP/IP, Ethernet, and broad networking concepts and some familiarity with the daily operation of networks. You should have programming experience in high-level programming and/or scripting languages (for example, C/C++, Java, or Python). Experiences with virtual machines and other virtual networking environments may also be useful. You will also need a computer with at least 1 GB (preferably more than 2 GB) of main memory and at least 10 GB of free hard disk space. A quite fast processor may speed up the boot time of virtual machines, and a big monitor may help to manage multiple terminal windows. You also need an Internet connection to download various utilities and VM images.

Who this book is for

Although this book covers the essential building blocks of OpenFlow and software-defined networking with OpenFlow, it is designed as a tutorial guide, and not a reference book. Network engineers, network administrators, systems software developers, and anyone who is interested in knowing more about OpenFlow, network application developers, are among the audiences of this book.

Conventions

In this book, you will find a number of styles of text that distinguish between different kinds of information. Here are some examples of these styles, and an explanation of their meaning.

Code words in text, database table names, folder names, filenames, file extensions, pathnames, dummy URLs, user input, and Twitter handles are shown as follows: "If a switch does not understand a vendor extension, it must send an `OFPT_ERROR` message with a `OFPET_BAD_REQUEST` error type, and a `OFPBRC_BAD_VENDOR` error code".

A block of code is set as follows:

```
class pyNetApp(Component):
def __init__(self, ctxt):

def learn_and_forward(self, dpid, inport, packet, buf, bufid):

self.send_openflow(dpid, bufid, buf, openflow.OFPP_FLOOD,inport)

if not packet.parsed:
log.debug('Ignoring incomplete packet.')
```

```
else:
self.learn_and_forward(dpid, inport, packet, packet.arr, bufid)
return CONTINUE
```

When we wish to draw your attention to a particular part of a code block, the relevant lines or items are set in bold:

```
attribs = {}
attribs[core.IN_PORT] = inport
attribs[core.DL_DST] = packet.dst
```

Any command-line input or output is written as follows:

```
# apt-get install maven git openjdk-7-jre openjdk-7-jdk
```

New terms and **important words** are shown in bold. Words that you see on the screen, in menus or dialog boxes for example, appear in the text like this: "Go to **File** and select **Import Appliance**".

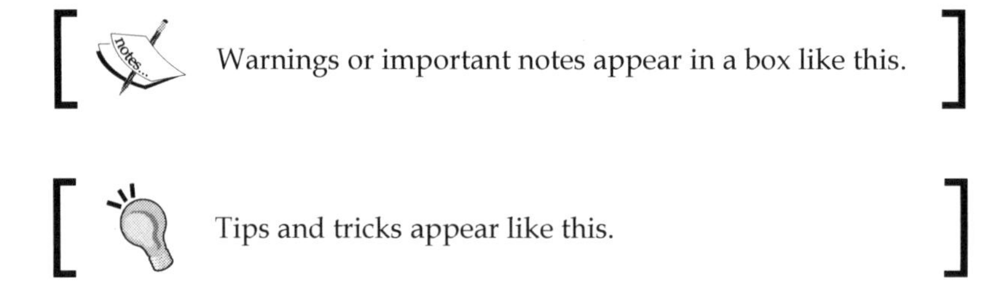

Reader feedback

Feedback from our readers is always welcome. Let us know what you think about this book—what you liked or may have disliked. Reader feedback is important for us to develop titles that you really get the most out of.

To send us general feedback, simply send an e-mail to `feedback@packtpub.com`, and mention the book title via the subject of your message.

If there is a topic that you have expertise in and you are interested in either writing or contributing to a book, see our author guide on `www.packtpub.com/authors`.

Customer support

Now that you are the proud owner of a Packt book, we have a number of things to help you to get the most from your purchase.

Downloading the example code

You can download the example code files for all Packt books you have purchased from your account at `http://www.packtpub.com`. If you purchased this book elsewhere, you can visit `http://www.packtpub.com/support` and register to have the files e-mailed directly to you.

Errata

Although we have taken every care to ensure the accuracy of our content, mistakes do happen. If you find a mistake in one of our books—maybe a mistake in the text or the code—we would be grateful if you would report this to us. By doing so, you can save other readers from frustration and help us improve subsequent versions of this book. If you find any errata, please report them by visiting `http://www.packtpub.com/submit-errata`, selecting your book, clicking on the **errata submission form** link, and entering the details of your errata. Once your errata are verified, your submission will be accepted and the errata will be uploaded on our website, or added to any list of existing errata, under the Errata section of that title. Any existing errata can be viewed by selecting your title from `http://www.packtpub.com/support`.

Piracy

Piracy of copyright material on the Internet is an ongoing problem across all media. At Packt, we take the protection of our copyright and licenses very seriously. If you come across any illegal copies of our works, in any form, on the Internet, please provide us with the location address or website name immediately so that we can pursue a remedy.

Please contact us at `copyright@packtpub.com` with a link to the suspected pirated material.

We appreciate your help in protecting our authors, and our ability to bring you valuable content.

Questions

You can contact us at `questions@packtpub.com` if you are having a problem with any aspect of the book, and we will do our best to address it.

1
Introducing OpenFlow

In order to understand the role of OpenFlow and its building blocks, and how it can be used for OpenFlow-based network application development, it is important to provide a brief introduction of OpenFlow and how it works. This chapter shapes the required knowledge prior to the actual setup of SDN/OpenFlow-enabled experimental and development environment. OpenFlow can be considered as one of the early implementations of the SDN concept. Therefore, before going through OpenFlow, it is worth giving a brief introduction to the SDN and the related activities around it.

Understanding Software Defined Networking – OpenFlow flavor

Software Defined Networking (**SDN**), often referred to as a *revolutionary new idea in computer networking*, promises to dramatically simplify network control, management, and enable innovation through network programmability. Computer networks are typically constructed from a large number of network devices (such as switches, routers, firewalls, and so on) with many complex protocols (software), which are implemented and embedded on them. Network engineers are responsible for configuring policies to respond to a wide range of network events and application scenarios. They manually transform these high-level policies into low-level configuration commands. These very complex tasks are often accomplished with access to very limited tools. Thus, network management control and performance tuning are quite challenging and error-prone tasks.

Another challenge is what network engineers and researchers refer to as *Internet ossification*. Due to its huge deployment base and its impacts on different aspects of our life, the Internet has become extremely difficult to evolve both in terms of its physical infrastructure, along with its protocols and performance. As emerging and demanding applications become more complex, the current status quo of the Internet seems not to be able to evolve to address emerging challenges.

The concept of *programmable networks* has been proposed as a way to facilitate network evolution. In particular, SDN is a new networking paradigm, in which the forwarding hardware (for example, specialized packet forwarding engines) is decoupled from the control decisions (for example, the protocols and control software). The migration of control logic, which used to be tightly integrated in the networking devices (for example, Ethernet switches) into accessible and logically centralized controllers, enables the underlying networking infrastructure to be *abstracted* from the application's point of view. This separation provides a more flexible, programmable, vendor-agnostic, cost efficient, and innovative network architecture. Besides the network abstraction, the SDN architecture will provide a set of **Application Programing Interfaces** (**APIs**) that simplifies the implementation of common network services (for example, routing, multicast, security, access control, bandwidth management, traffic engineering, QoS, energy efficiency, and various forms of policy management). In SDN, the network intelligence is logically centralized in software-based controllers (at the control plane), and network devices become the simple packet forwarding devices (the data plane) that can be programmed via an open interface. One of the early implementations of this open interface is called OpenFlow.

The separation of the forwarding hardware from the control logic allows easier deployment of new protocols and applications, straightforward network visualization and management, and consolidation of various middle boxes into software control. Instead of enforcing policies and running protocols on a convolution of scattered devices, the network is reduced to *simple* forwarding hardware and the decision-making network controller(s). The forwarding hardware consists of the following:

1. A flow table containing flow entries consisting of match rules and actions that take on active flows.
2. A transport layer protocol that securely communicates with a controller about new entries that are not currently in the flow table.

Activities around SDN/OpenFlow

While OpenFlow has received a considerable amount of industry attention, it is worth mentioning that the idea of programmable networks and decoupled control plane (control logic) from data plane has been around for many years. The **Open Signaling Working Group** (**OPENSIG**) initiated a series of workshops in 1995 to make ATM, Internet, and mobile networks more open, extensible, and programmable. Motivated by these ideas, an **Internet Engineering Task Force** (**IETF**) working group came up with **General Switch Management Protocol** (**GSMP**), to control a label switch. This group is officially concluded and GSMPv3 was published in June, 2002. The **Active**

Network initiative proposed the idea of a network infrastructure that would be programmable for customized services. However, Active Network never gathered critical mass, mainly due to practical security and performance concerns. Starting in 2004, the 4D project (`www.cs.cmu.edu/~4D/`) advocated a clean slate design that emphasized separation between the routing decision logic and the protocols governing the interaction between network elements. The ideas in the 4D project provided direct inspiration for later works such as NOX (`www.noxrepo.org`), which proposed an *operating system for networks* in the context of an OpenFlow-enabled network. Later on in 2006, the IETF **Network Configuration Protocol** working group proposed **NETCONF** as a management protocol for modifying the configuration of network devices. The working group is currently active and the latest proposed standard was published in June, 2011. The IETF **Forwarding and Control Element Separation (ForCES)** working group is leading a parallel approach to SDN. SDN and **Open Networking Foundation** share some common goals with ForCES. With ForCES, the internal network device architecture is redefined as the control element is separated from the forwarding element, but the combined entity is still represented as a single network element to the outside world. The immediate predecessor to OpenFlow was the Stanford's **SANE/Ethane** project (`yuba.stanford.edu/sane`, and `yuba.stanford.edu/ethane/`), which, in 2006, defined a new network architecture for enterprise networks. Ethane's focus was on using a centralized controller to manage policy and security in a network.

> A group of network operators, service providers, and vendors have recently created the Open Networking Foundation (`www.opennetworking.org`), an industrial driven organization, to promote SDN and standardize the OpenFlow protocol. At the time of writing this, the latest specification of OpenFlow was version 1.4. However, since the widely implemented and deployed specification is OpenFlow 1.0.0 (Wire Protocol `0x01`), we will limit ourselves to the OpenFlow 1.0.0 in this book.

Building Blocks

The SDN switch (for instance, an OpenFlow switch), the SDN controller, and the interfaces present on the controller for communication with forwarding devices, generally southbound interface (OpenFlow) and network applications interface (northbound interface) are the fundamental building blocks of an SDN deployment. Switches in an SDN are often represented as basic forwarding hardware accessible via an open interface, as the control logic and algorithms are offloaded to a controller. OpenFlow switches come in two varieties: pure (OpenFlow-only) and hybrid (OpenFlow-enabled).

Pure OpenFlow switches have no legacy features or on-board control, and completely rely on a controller for forwarding decisions. Hybrid switches support OpenFlow in addition to traditional operation and protocols. Most commercial switches available today are hybrids. An OpenFlow switch consists of a flow table, which performs packet lookup and forwarding. Each flow table in the switch holds a set of flow entries that consists of:

1. Header fields or match fields, with information found in packet header, ingress port, and metadata, used to match incoming packets.
2. Counters, used to collect statistics for the particular flow, such as number of received packets, number of bytes, and duration of the flow.
3. A set of instructions or actions to be applied after a match that dictates how to handle matching packets. For instance, the action might be to forward a packet out to a specified port.

The decoupled system in SDN (and OpenFlow) can be compared to an application program and an operating system in a computing platform. In SDN, the controller (that is, network operating system) provides a programmatic interface to the network, where applications can be written to perform control and management tasks, and offer new functionalities. A layered view of this model is illustrated in the following figure. This view assumes that the control is centralized and applications are written as if the network is a single system. While this simplifies policy enforcement and management tasks, the bindings must be closely maintained between the control and the network forwarding elements. As shown in the following figure, a controller that strives to act as a network operating system must implement at least two interfaces: a *southbound* interface (for example, OpenFlow) that allows switches to communicate with the controller and a *northbound* interface that presents a programmable API to network control and high-level policy applications/services. Header fields (match fields) are shown in the following figure. Each entry of the flow table contains a specific value, or ANY (* or wildcard, as depicted in the following figure), which matches any value.

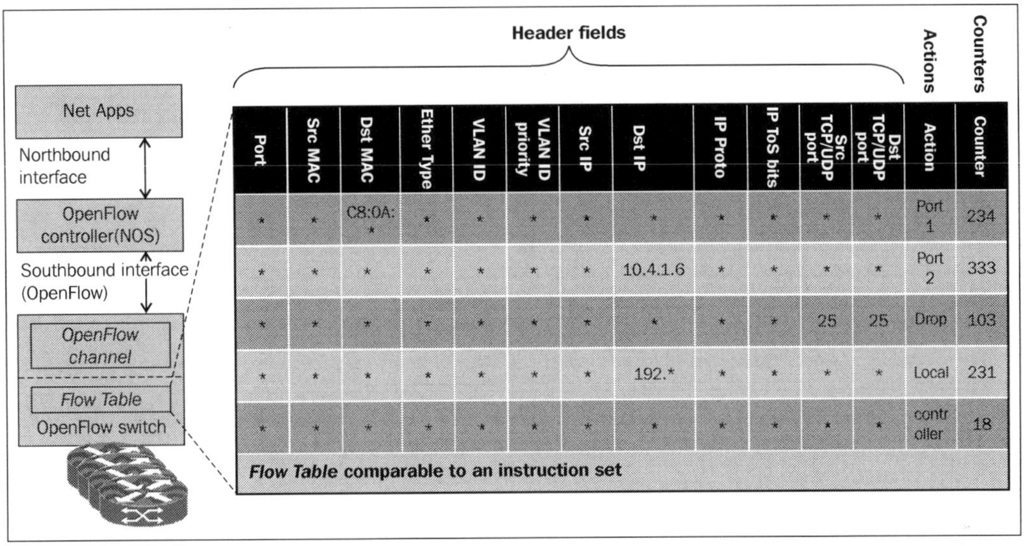

Net Apps
Northbound interface
OpenFlow controller(NOS)
Southbound interface (OpenFlow)
OpenFlow channel
Flow Table
OpenFlow switch

Header fields | Actions | Counters

Port	Src MAC	Dst MAC	Ether Type	VLAN ID	VLAN ID priority	Src IP	Dst IP	IP Proto	IP ToS bits	Src TCP/UDP port	Dst TCP/UDP port	Action	Counter
*	*	C8:0A:*	*	*	*	*	*	*	*	*	*	Port 1	234
*	*	*	*	*	*	*	10.4.1.6	*	*	*	*	Port 2	333
*	*	*	*	*	*	*	*	*	*	25	25	Drop	103
*	*	*	*	*	*	*	192.*	*	*	*	*	Local	231
*	*	*	*	*	*	*	*	*	*	*	*	controller	18

Flow Table comparable to an instruction set

OpenFlow switch, Flow table, OpenFlow controller, and network applications.

If the switch supports subnet masks on the IP source and/or destination fields, these can more precisely specify matches. The port field (or ingress port) numerically represents the incoming port of the switch and starts at 1. The length of this field is implementation dependent. The ingress port field is applicable to all packets. The source and destination MAC (Ethernet) addresses are applicable to all packets on enabled ports of the switch and their length is 48 bits. The Ethernet type field is 16 bits wide and is applicable to all the packets on enabled ports. An OpenFlow switch must match the type in both standard Ethernet and IEEE 802.2 with a **Subnetwork Access Protocol (SNAP)** header and **Organizationally Unique Identifier (OUI)** of `0x000000`. The special value of `0x05FF` is used to match all the 802.3 packets without SNAP headers. VLAN ID is applicable to all packets with and Ethernet type of `0x8100`. The size of this field is 12 bits (that is, 4096 VLANs). The VLAN priority (or the VLAN PCP field) is 3 bits wide and is applicable to all packets of Ethernet type `0x8100`. The IP source and destination address fields are 32 bit entities and are applicable to all IP and ARP packets. These fields can be masked with a subnet mask. The IP protocol field is applicable to all IP, IP over Ethernet, an the ARP packets. Its length is 8 bits and in case of ARP packets, only the lower 8 bits of the ARP op-code are used. The IP **ToS (Type of Service)** bits has a length of 6 bits and is applicable to all IP packets. It specifies an 8 bit value and places ToS in the upper 6 bits. The source and destination transport port addresses (or ICMP type/code) have a length of 16 bits and are applicable to all TCP, UDP, and ICMP packets. In case of the ICMP type/code only the lower 8 bits are considered for matching.

Counters are maintained per table, per flow, per port and per queue. Counters wrap around with no overflow indicator. The required set of counters is summarized in the following figure. The phrase byte in this figure (and throughout this book) refers to an 8 bit octet. Duration refers to the time the flow has been installed in the flow table of the switch. The receive errors field includes all explicitly specified errors, including frame, overrun, and CRC errors, plus any others.

Per Port Counters:

Received Packets (64 bits)
Transmitted Packets (64 bits)
Received Bytes (64 bits)
Transmitted Bytes (64 bits)
Receive Drops (64 bits)
Transmit Drops (64 bits)
Receive Errors (64 bits)
Transmit Errors (64 bits)
Receive Frame Alignment Errors (64 bits)
Receive Overrun Errors (64 bits)
Receive CRC Errors (64 bits)
Collisions (64 bits)

Per Table Counters:

Active Entries (32 bits)
Packt lookups (64 bits)
Packet Matches (64 bits)

Per Flow Counters:

Received Packets (64 bits)
Received Bytes (64 bits)
Duration (seconds) (32 bits)
Duration (nano seconds) (32 bits)

Per Queue Counters:

Transmitted Packets (64 bits)
Transmitted Bytes (64 bits)
Transmit Overrun Errors (64 bits)

Required list of counters for use in statistical messages.

Each flow entry is associated with zero or more actions that instruct the OpenFlow switch how to handle matching packets. If no forward actions are present, the packet is dropped. Action lists must be processed in the specified order. However, there is no guaranteed packet output ordering within an individual port. For instance, two packets which are generated and destined to a single output port as part of the action processing, may be arbitrarily re-ordered. Pure OpenFlow switches only support the *Required Actions*, while hybrid OpenFlow switches may also support the **NORMAL** action. Either type of switches can also support the **FLOOD** action. The *Required Actions* are:

- **Forward**: OpenFlow switches must support forwarding the packet to physical ports and the following virtual ones:
    - **ALL**: Send the packet on to all interfaces, excluding the incoming port
    - **CONTROLLER**: Encapsulate and send the packet to the controller
    - **LOCAL**: Send the packet to the local networking stack of the switch
    - **TABLE** (Only for packet-out message): Perform action in the flow table
    - **IN_PORT**: Send the packet out the input port

- **Drop**: This indicates that all the matching packets should be dropped. A flow entry with no specified action is considered as a Drop action.
- The *Optional Actions* are:
    - **Forward**: A switch may optionally support the following virtual ports for forward action:

      NORMAL: Process the packet using the traditional forwarding path supported by the switch (that is traditional L2, VLAN, and/or L3 processing)

      FLOOD: Flood the packet along the minimum spanning tree, not including the incoming interface.
- **Enqueue**: This forwards a packet through a queue attached to a port. Forwarding behavior is dictated by the configuration of the queue and is used to provide the basic QoS support.
- **Modify field**: The optional (recommended) field modification actions are:
    - Setting VLAN ID: If no VLAN is present, a new header is added with the specified VLAN ID (12 bit associated data) and priority of zero. If a VLAN header already exists, the VLAN ID is replaced with the specified value.
    - Setting VLAN priority: If no VLAN is present, a new header is added with the specified priority (3 bit associated data) and VLAN ID of zero. If a VLAN ID header already exists, the priority field is replaced with the specified value.
    - Striping the VLAN header: This Strip VLAN header if present.
    - Modifying the Ethernet source/destination MAC address: This replaces the existing Ethernet source/destination MAC address with the new value (specified as a 48 bits data).
    - Modifying the IPv4 source/destination address: This replaces the existing IP source/destination address with a new value (associated with a 32 bits data) and updates the IP checksum (and TCP/UDP checksum if applicable). This action is only applicable to IPv4 packets.
    - Modifying the IPv4 ToS bits: This replace the existing IP ToS field with the 6 bits associated data. This action is only applicable to IPv4 packets.
    - Modifying the transport source/destination port: This replaces the existing TCP/UDP source/destination port with associated 16 bits data and updates the TCP/UDP checksum. This action is only applicable to TCP and UDP packets.

Upon a packet arrival at the OpenFlow switch, the packet header fields are extracted and matched against the matching fields' portion of the flow table entries. This matching starts at the first flow table entry and continues through subsequent flow table entries. If a matching entry is found, the switch applies the appropriate set of instructions associated with the matched flow entry. For each packet that matches a flow entry, the associated counters for that entry are updated. If the flow table look-up procedure does not result on a match, the action taken by the switch will depend on the instructions defined at the table-miss flow entry. The flow table must contain a table-miss entry in order to handle table misses. This particular entry specifies a set of actions to be performed when no match is found for an incoming packet. These actions include dropping the packet, sending the packet out on all interfaces, or forwarding the packet to the controller over the secure OpenFlow channel. Header fields used for the table lookup depend on the packet types as described below:

- Rules specifying a port (ingress port) are matched against the physical port that received the packet.
- The Ethernet headers (Source MAC, Destination MAC, Ethernet Type, and more) as specified in the first figure, and are used for all packets.
- If the packet is a VLAN (Ethernet type `0x8100`), the VLAN ID and VLAN priority (PCP) fields are used in the lookup.
- For IP packets (Ethernet type equal to `0x0800`), the lookup fields also include those in the IP header (Source IP, Destination IP, IP protocol, ToS, and so on).
- For IP packets that are TCP or UDP (IP protocol equal to 6 or 17), the lookup includes the transport ports (TCP/UDP source/destination ports).
- For IP packets that are ICMP (IP protocol equal to 1), the lookup includes the Type and Code fields.
- For IP packets with nonzero fragment offset or more fragments bit set, the transport ports are set to zero for the lookup.
- Optionally, for ARP packets (Ethernet type equal to `0x0806`), the lookup fields may also include the contained IP source and destination fields.

Packets are matched against flow entries based on prioritization. An entry that specifies an exact match (that is no wildcards) is always the highest priority. All wildcard entries have a priority associated with them. Higher priority entries must match before lower priority ones. If multiple entries have the same priority, the switch is free to choose any ordering. Higher numbers have higher priorities. The following figure shows the packet flow in an OpenFlow switch. It is important to note that if a flow table field has a value of ANY (*, wildcard), it matches all the possible values in the header.

There are various Ethernet framing types (Ethernet II, 802.3 with or without SNAP, and so on). If the packet is an Ethernet II frame, the Ethernet type is handled in the expected way. If the packet is an 802.3 frame with a SNAP header and an OUI equal to `0x000000`, the SNAP protocol ID is matched against the flow's Ethernet type. A flow entry that specified an Ethernet Type of `0x05FF`, matches all Ethernet 802.2 frames without a SNAP header and those with SNAP headers that do not have an OUI of `0x000000`.

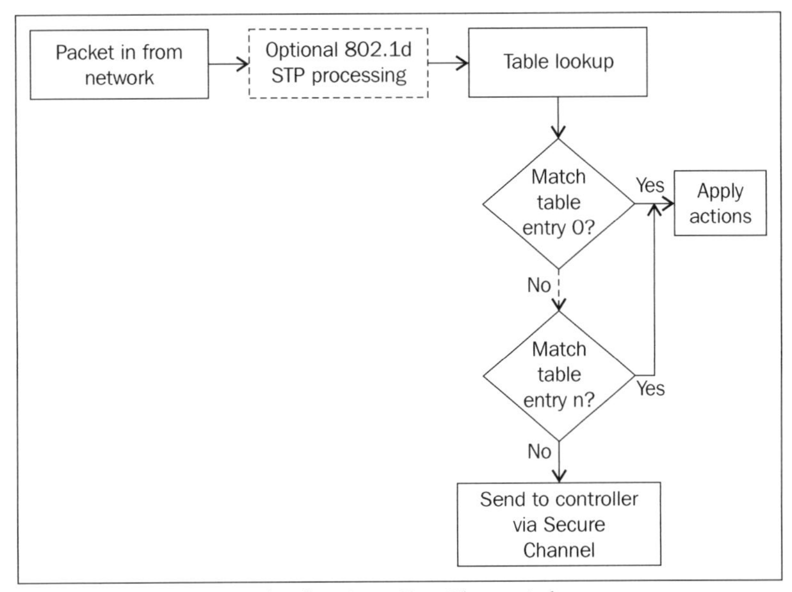

Packet flow in an OpenFlow switch.

OpenFlow messages

The communication between the controller and switch happens using the OpenFlow protocol, where a set of defined messages can be exchanged between these entities over a secure channel. The secure channel is the interface that connects each OpenFlow switch to a controller. The **Transport Layer Security** (**TLS**) connection to the user-defined (otherwise fixed) controller is initiated by the switch on its power on. The controller's default TCP port is `6633`. The switch and controller mutually authenticate by exchanging certificates signed by a site-specific private key. Each switch must be user-configurable with one certificate for authenticating the controller (controller certificate) and the other for authenticating to the controller (switch certificate).

Traffic to and from the secure channel is not checked against the flow table and therefore the switch must identify incoming traffic as local before checking it against the flow table. In the case that a switch loses contact with the controller, as a result of an echo request timeout, TLS session timeout, or other disconnection, it should attempt to contact one or more backup controllers. If some number of attempts to contact a controller (zero or more) fail, the switch must enter *emergency mode* and immediately reset the current TCP connection. Then the matching process is dictated by the emergency flow table entries (marked with the emergency bit set). Emergency flow modify messages must have timeout value set to zero. Otherwise, the switch must refuse the addition and respond with an error message. All normal entries are deleted when entering emergency mode. Upon connecting to a controller again, the emergency flow entries remain. The controller then has the option of deleting all the flow entries, if desired.

The first time a switch boots up, it is considered to be in emergency mode. Configuration of the default set of flow entries is outside the scope of the OpenFlow protocol.

The controller configures and manages the switch, receives events from the switch, and sends packets out to the switch through this interface. Using the OpenFlow protocol, a remote controller can add, update, or delete flow entries from the switch's flow table. That can happen reactively (in response to a packet arrival) or proactively. The OpenFlow protocol can be viewed as one possible implementation of controller-switch interactions (southbound interface), as it defines the communication between the switching hardware and a network controller. For security, OpenFlow 1.3.x provides optional support for encrypted TLS communication and a certificate exchange between the switches/controller(s); however, the exact implementation and certificate format is not currently specified. Also, fine-grained security options regarding scenarios with multiple controllers are outside the scope of the current specification, as there is no specific method to only grant partial access permissions to an authorized controller. The OpenFlow protocol defines three message types, each with multiple subtypes:

- Controller-to-switch
- Symmetric
- Asynchronous

Controller-to-switch

Controller-to-switch messages are initiated by the controller and used to directly manage or inspect the state of the switch. This type of messages may or may not require a response from the switch and are categorized in the following subtypes.

Features

Upon establishment of the TLS session, the controller sends a feature request message to the switch. The switch must reply with a *features reply* message that specifies the features and capabilities that are supported by the switch.

Configuration

The controller is able to set and query configuration parameters in the switch. The switch only responds to a query from the controller.

Modify-State

These messages are sent by the controller to manage the state of the switches. They are used to add/delete or modify flow table entries or to set switch port priorities. Flow table modification messages can have the following types:

- **ADD**: For the `ADD` requests with the `OFPFF_CHECK_OVERLAP` flag set, the switch must first check for any overlapping flow entries. Two flow entries overlap if a single packet may match both, and both entries have the same priority. If an overlap conflict exists between an existing flow entry and the `ADD` request, the switch must refuse the addition and respond with `ofp_error_msg` with the `OFPET_FLOW_MODE_FAILED` error type and the `OFPFMFC_OVERLAP` error code. For the valid (non-overlapping) `ADD` requests, or those with no overlap checking flag set, the switch must insert the flow entry at the lowest numbered table entry for which the switch supports all wildcards set in the `flow_match` struct, and for which the priority would be observed during the matching process. If a flow entry with identical header fields and priority already resides in the flow table, then that entry including its counters must be removed and the new flow entry must be added. If a switch cannot find any table entry to add the incoming flow entry, the switch should send `ofp_error_msg` with the `OFPET_FLOW_MOD_FAILD` type and the `PFOFMFC_ALL_TABLES_FULL` error code. If the action list in a flow modify message references a port that will never be valid on a switch, the switch must return `ofp_error_msg` with the `OFPET_BAD_ACTION` type and the `OFPBAC_BAD_OUT` code. If the referenced port may be valid in the future (for example, when a line card is added to a chassis) the switch may either silently drop packets sent to the referenced port, or immediately return an `OFPBAC_BAD_PORT` error and refuse the flow modify message.

- **MODIFY**: If a flow entry with an identical header field does not currently reside in the flow table, the `MODIFY` command acts like an `ADD` command, and the new flow entry must be inserted with zeroed counters. Otherwise the actions field is changed on the existing entry and its counters and idle timeout fields are left unchanged.
- **DELETE**: For delete requests, if no flow entry matches, no error is recorded and no flow table modification occurs. If a flow entry matches, the entry must be deleted, and then each normal entry with the `OFPFF_SEND_FLOW_REM` flag set should generate a flow removal message. Deleted emergency flow entries generate no flow removal messages. `DELETE` and `DELETE_STRICT` (see next bullet point) commands can be optionally filtered by the output port. If the `out_port` field contains a value other than `OFPP_NONE`, it introduces a constraint when matching. This constraint is that the rule must contain an output action directed at that port. This field is ignored by the `ADD`, `MODIFY`, and `MODIFY_STRICT` messages.
- **MODIFY** and **DELETE**: These flow mode commands have corresponding `_STRICT` versions. In non-`RESTRICT` versions, the wildcards are active and all flows that match the description are modified or removed. In `_STRICT` versions, all fields, including the wildcards and priority, are strictly matched against the entry and only an identical flow is modified or removed. For instance, if a message to remove entries is sent to the switch that has all wildcard flags set, the `DELETE` command would delete all flows from all tables. However, the `DELETE_STRICT` command would only delete a rule that applies to all packets at the specified priority. For the non-strict `MODIFY` and `DELETE` commands that contain wildcards, a match will occur when a flow entry exactly matches or is more specific than the description in the `flow_mod` command. For example, if a `DELETE` command says to delete all flows with a destination port of `80`, then a flow entry that has all wildcards will not be deleted. However, a `DELETE` command that has all wildcards will delete an entry that matches all port `80` traffic.

Read-State

These messages collect statistics from the switch flow tables, ports, and the individual flow entries.

Send-Packet

These are used by the controller to send packets out of a specified port on the switch.

Barrier

Barrier request/reply messages are used by the controller to ensure message dependencies have been met or to receive notifications for completed operations.

Symmetric messages

Symmetric messages are initiated by either the switch or the controller and sent without solicitation. There are three symmetric message subtypes in OpenFlow protocol as follows:

Hello

Hello messages are exchanged between the switch and controller upon connection setup.

Echo

Echo request/reply messages can be sent from either the switch or the controller, and must return an echo reply. These messages can be used to indicate the latency, bandwidth, and/or liveliness of a controller-switch connection (that is a heartbeat).

Vendor

These messages provide a standard way for OpenFlow switches to offer additional functionality within the OpenFlow message type space for future revisions of OpenFlow.

Asynchronous messages

Asynchronous messages are initiated by the switch and used to update the controller of network events and changes to the switch state. Switches send asynchronous messages to the controller to denote a packet arrival, switch state change, or an error. There are four main asynchronous messages as follows:

Packet-in

For all packets that do not have a matching flow entry or if a packet matches an entry with a *send to controller* action, a packet-in message is sent to the controller. If the switch has sufficient memory to buffer packets that are sent to the controller, the packet-in message contains some fraction of the packet header (by default, 128 bytes) and a buffer ID to be used by the controller when it is ready for the switch to forward the packet. Switches that do not support internal buffering (or have run out of internal buffer space) must send the full packet to the controller as part of the message.

Flow-Removal

When a flow entry is added to the switch by a flow modify message (the *Modify State* section), an idle timeout value indicates when the entry should be removed due to the lack of activity as well as a hard timeout value. The hard timeout value indicates when the entry should be removed, regardless of activity. The flow modify message also specifies whether the switch should send a flow removal message to the controller when the flow expires. Flow modify messages, which delete flow entries may also cause flow removal messages.

Port-status

The switch is expected to send port-status messages to the controller as the port configuration state changes. These events include changes in port status (for example, disabled by the user) or a change in the port status as specified by 802.1D (Spanning Tree). OpenFlow switches may optionally support 802.1D **Spanning Tree Protocol** (**STP**).These switches are expected to process all 802.1D packets locally before performing flow lookup. Ports status as specified by the STP is then used to limit packets forwarded to the `OFP_FLOOD` port to only those ports along the spanning tree. Port changes as a result of the spanning tree are sent to the controller via the port-update messages. Note that forward actions that specify the outgoing port of `OFP_ALL` ignore the port status set by the STP. Packets received on the ports that are disabled by the STP must follow the normal flow table processing path.

Error

The switch is able to notify the controller of problems using error messages.

The heart of OpenFlow specification is the set of C structures used for OpenFlow protocol messages. Interested readers can find these data structures and their detailed explanation available at:

`www.openflow.org/documents/openflow-spec-v1.0.0.pdf` or `www.opennetworking.org/sdn-resources/onf-specifications`.

Northbound interface

External management systems or network applications (Net Apps) may wish to extract information about the underlying network or control an aspect of the network behavior or policy. Additionally, controllers may find it necessary to communicate with each other for a variety of reasons. For instance, an internal control application may need to reserve resources across multiple domains of control, or a primary controller may need to share policy information with a backup controller. Unlike controller-switch communication (that is the southbound interface), there is no currently accepted standard for northbound interface and they are more likely to be implemented on an *ad-hoc* basis for particular applications. One potential reason is that the northbound interface is defined entirely in software, while controller-switch interactions must enable the hardware implementation. If we consider the controller as a *network operating system*, then there should be a clearly defined interface by which applications can access the underlying hardware (switches), coexist and interact with other applications, and utilize system services (for example, topology discovery, forwarding, and so on), without requiring the application developer to know the implementation details of the controller (that is the network operating system). While there are several controllers that exist, their application interfaces are still in the early stages and independent from each other and incompatible. Until a clear northbound interface standard emerges, SDN applications will continue to be developed in an *ad-hoc* fashion and the concept of flexible and portable *network apps* may have to wait for some time.

Summary

The OpenFlow is the continuation of many previous efforts to provide decoupled control and data forwarding in networking equipment. A background of these efforts was presented in this chapter. Presenting the key building blocks of an SDN deployment, in particular the OpenFlow protocol and its basic operation were covered in this chapter. After introducing OpenFlow, in the next chapter we present the reference implementation of OpenFlow switch in software and hardware along with an introduction to Mininet experiment environment.

2
Implementing the OpenFlow Switch

In this chapter we will be covering implementation of the OpenFlow switch (v1.0) and important hardware and software OpenFlow switches. Then we will introduce Mininet as an integrated environment to experience with the OpenFlow switches and controllers. The reference implementation of OpenFlow and hardware/software products will be presented in this chapter. An OpenFlow laboratory using Mininet network emulation is explained along with a step-by-step experiment in Mininet.

OpenFlow reference switch

OpenFlow switch is a basic forwarding element, which is accessible via OpenFlow protocol and interface. Although at first glance this setup would appear to simplify the switching hardware, flow-based SDN architectures such as OpenFlow may require additional forwarding table entries, buffer space, and statistical counters that are not very easy to implement in traditional switches with **application specific ICs** (**ASICs**). In an OpenFlow network, switches come in two flavors, hybrid (OpenFlow enabled) and pure (OpenFlow only). Hybrid switches support OpenFlow in addition to traditional operation and protocols (L2/L3 switching). Pure OpenFlow switches have no legacy features or onboard control, and completely rely on a controller for forwarding decisions. Most of the currently available and commercial switches are hybrids. Since OpenFlow switches are controlled by an open interface (over TCP-based TLS session), it is important that this link remains available and secure. The OpenFlow protocol can be viewed as one possible implementation of SDN-based controller-switch interactions (which is a messaging protocol), as it defines the communication between the OpenFlow switch and an OpenFlow controller.

The reference implementation of the OpenFlow switch from Stanford University includes `ofdatapath`, which implements the flow table in user space; `ofprotocol`, a program that implements the secure channel component of the reference switch; and `dpctl`, which is a tool for configuring the switch. This distribution includes some additional software as well (for instance, `controller`, a simple controller program that connects to any number of OpenFlow switches and a Wireshark dissector that can decode the OpenFlow protocol). The following figure depicts the OpenFlow reference switch, interface, and three message types (controller-to-switch, asynchronous, and symmetric) and sub-types. These messages were briefly introduced in the previous chapter. They are presented with more implementation related details in this section. Controller-to-switch messages are initiated by the controller and may or may not require a response from the OpenFlow switch.

OpenFlow 1.3.0 provides optional support for encrypted TLS communication and a certificate exchange between the OpenFlow switches/controller(s). However, the exact implementation and certificate format is not currently specified. Furthermore, fine-grained security options regarding scenarios with multiple OpenFlow controllers are out of the scope of the current OpenFlow specification. There is no method specified to only grant partial access permissions to an authorized OpenFlow controller. Also note that in this book we strictly stick to OpenFlow 1.0.0 specification. The reference OpenFlow 1.0.0 implementation can be downloaded from: `www.openflow.org/wp/downloads/`

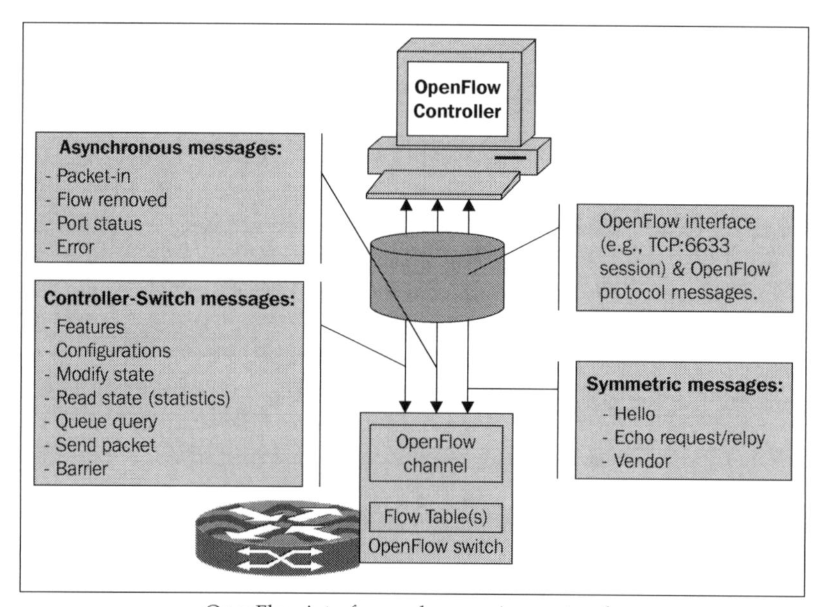

OpenFlow interface and messaging protocol.

These messages are used to directly manage or inspect the state of the switch:

- **Features**: Upon the establishment of the TLS session (for example, TCP TLS session on port `6633`), the controller sends an `OFPT_FEATURES_REQUEST` message to the switch and the OpenFlow switch reports back (via `OFPT_FEATURES_REPLY` message) the features and capabilities that it has and supports. The datapath identifier (`datapath_id`), number of supported flow tables by data path (OpenFlow switch), switch capabilities, supported actions, and definition of ports are the important features that are reported to the controller. The `datapath_id` field uniquely identifies an OpenFlow switch (data path). It is a 64-bit entity and the lower 48 bits are intended for the switch MAC address, while the top 16 bits are up to the manufacturers.
- **Configuration**: The controller is able to set and query configuration parameters in the switch with the `OFPT_SET_CONFIG` and `OFPT_GET_CONFIG_REPLY` messages, respectively. The switch responds to a configuration request with an `OFPT_GET_CONFIG_REPLY` message; it does not reply to a request to set the configuration.
- **Modify state**: Modifications to the flow table from the controller are done with the `OFPT_FLOW_MOD` message and the controller uses the `OFPT_PORT_MOD` message to modify the behavior of the physical ports. The flow modification commands are `ADD`, `MODIFY`, `MODIFY_STRICT`, `DELETE`, and `DELETE_STRICT`, which were explained in *Chapter 1, Introducing OpenFlow*. The port configuration bits indicate whether a port has been administratively brought down, options for handling 802.1D **spanning tree protocol** (**STP**) packets, and how to handle incoming and outgoing packets. The controller may set `OFPPFL_NO_STP` to `0` to enable STP on a port, or to `1` to disable STP on a port. The OpenFlow reference implementation sets this bit to `0` (enabling STP) by default.
- **Read State (Statistics)**: The controller can query the status of the switch using `OFPT_STAT_REQUEST` message. The switch responds with one or more `OFPT_STATS_REPLY` messages. There is a `type` field in these message exchanges, which specifies the kind of information that is being exchanged (OpenFlow switch description, individual flow statistics, aggregate flow statistics, flow table statistics, physical port statistics, queue statistics for a port, and vendor-specific messages) and determines how the body field should be interpreted.

- **Queue query**: An OpenFlow switch provides limited **Quality of Service** (**QoS**) support through a simple queuing mechanism. One (or more) queue(s) can be attached to a port and could be used to map flows on it (them). The flows, which are mapped to a specific queue, will be treated according to the configuration of that queue (for example, minimum rate control). Note that queue configuration takes place outside the OpenFlow protocol (for example, through command-line interface) or an external dedicated configuration protocol. The controller can query the switch for configured queues on a port using queue query message.
- **Send packet**: Using this message (that is, `OFPT_PACKET_OUT`), the controller is able to send packets out of a specified port of the OpenFlow switch.
- **Barrier**: This message is sent whenever the controller wants to ensure message dependencies have been met or wants to receive notifications for completed operations. The message is `OFPT_BARRIER_REQUEST` and has no message body. Upon receipt, the OpenFlow switch must finish processing all previously-received messages before executing any message beyond the barrier request. When current processing is completed, the switch must send an `OFPT_BARRIER_REPLY` message the transaction ID (`xid`) of the original request.

Asynchronous messages

Asynchronous messages are initiated by the switch, used to update the controller of network events, and changes to the switch state. Switches send asynchronous messages to the controller to denote a packet arrival, flow removal, port status change, or an error.

When packets are received by the switch (data path), they are sent to the controller using the `OFPT_PACKET_IN` message. When a packet is buffered in the switch, some number of bytes from the message will be included in the data portion of the message. If the packet is sent because of a send-to-controller action, then the `max_len` bytes are sent and if the packet is sent due to a flow table miss, then at least the `miss_send_len` bytes are sent. If the packet is not buffered inside the switch, then the entire packet is included in the data portion of the message. Switches that implement buffering are expected to expose the amount of buffering and the length of time before buffers may be reused. An OpenFlow switch must gracefully handle the case where a buffered `packet_in` message gets no response from the controller.

When flows time out, the OpenFlow switch notifies the controller with OFPT_FLOW_REMOVED message (if the controller has requested to be notified). The duration_sec and duration_nsec fields of the message indicate the elapsed time the flow has been installed in the switch. The total duration in nanoseconds can be computed as duration_sec x 10^9 + duration_nanosec. Implementations are required to provide millisecond precision. The idle_timeout field is directly extracted from the FLOW_MOD that created the flow table entry.

As physical ports are added, modified, and possibly removed from the data path, the controller needs to be informed with the OPFT_PORT_STATUS message. Also there are cases where the OpenFlow switch needs to notify the controller of a problem. The message includes an error type, error code, and a variable-length data that should be interpreted according to the error type and code. In most cases, the data part is the message that caused the problem. There are six types of error. OFPET_HELLO_FAILED indicates that Hello protocol failed. OFPET_BAD_REQUEST refers to the case, where the request was not understood. Error in action description is indicated by OFPET_BAD_ACTION. If the FLOW_MOD or PORT_MOD requests are failed then the error type is OFPET_FLOW_MOD_FAILED and OFPET_PORT_MOD_FAILED, respectively. Failure in port queue operations is classified with OFPET_QUEUE_OP_FAILED.

Symmetric Messages

The hello message (OFPT_HELLO), echo request/reply, and vendor message are symmetric OpenFlow messages. In the OpenFlow reference implementation that includes a user space process and a kernel module, echo request/reply is implemented in the kernel module. This implementation consideration provides more accurate end-to-end latency timing. The vendor field in the OFPT_VENDOR message is a 32-bit value that uniquely identifies the vendor. If the most significant byte is zero, the next three bytes (24 bits) are the vendor's IEEE OUI. If a switch does not understand a vendor extension, it must send an OFPT_ERROR message with a OFPET_BAD_REQUEST error type, and a OFPBRC_BAD_VENDOR error code.

Hardware Implementations

OpenFlow reference standard (OpenFlow 1.0.0, Wire Protocol 0x01) is the main and early SDN enabling technologies being currently implemented in the commodity-networking hardware. In this section, we do not intend to give a complete detailed overview of OpenFlow enabled switches and manufacturers, but rather give a brief list of a few options that are available in the market.

The following table lists commercial switches that are currently available, along with their manufacturer, and the version of OpenFlow they have implemented:

Manufacturer	Switch models	OpenFlow version
Brocade	NetIron CES 2000 Series, CER 2000,	1.0
Hewlett Packard	3500/3500yl, 5400zl,6200zl, 6600, 8200zl	1.0
IBM	RackSwitch G8264, G8264T	1.0
Juniper	EX9200 Programmable switch	1.0
NEC	PF5240, PF5820	1.0
Pica8	P-3290, P-3295, P-3780, P3920	1.2
Pronto	3290 and 3780	1.0
Broadcom	BCM56846	1.0
Extreme Networks	BlackDiamond 8K, Summit X440, X460, X480	1.0
Netgear	GSM7352Sv2	1.0
Arista	7150, 7500, 7050 series	1.0

Software-based switches

There are currently several OpenFlow software switches available that can be used, for instance, to run an OpenFlow test-bed or to develop and test OpenFlow-based network applications. A list of current software switches with a brief description, including implementation language and the OpenFlow standard, are as follows:

- **Open vSwitch**: This is a multilayer and production quality virtual switch licensed under the Apache 2.0 license. It is designed to enable network automation through programmatic extension, while still supporting standard management interfaces and protocols (for example, NetFlow, sFlow, OpenFlow, OVSDB, and so on.).
- **Indigo**: This is an open source OpenFlow implementation that runs on physical switches and uses the hardware features of Ethernet switch ASICs to run OpenFlow at line rates. It is based on the OpenFlow Reference Implementation from Stanford University.

- **LINC**: This is an open source project led by FlowForwarding effort and is an Apache 2 license implementation based on OpenFlow 1.2/1.3.1. LINC is architected to use generally-available commodity x86 hardware and runs on a variety of platforms such as Linux, Solaris, Windows, MacOS, and FreeBSD where Erlang runtime is available.
- **Pantou (OpenWRT)**: This turns a commercial wireless router/access point to an OpenFlow-enabled switch. OpenFlow is implemented as an application on top of OpenWrt. Pantou is based on the BackFire OpenWrt release (Linux 2.6.32). The OpenFlow module is based on the Stanford reference implementation (userspace). At the time of this writing, it supports generic Broadcom and some models of LinkSys and TP-LINK access points with Broadcom and Atheros chipsets.
- **Of13softswtich**: This is an OpenFlow 1.3 compatible user-space software switch implementation based on the Ericsson TrafficLab 1.1 softswitch. The latest version of this software switch includes the switch implementation (`ofdatapath`), a secure channel for connecting the switch to the controller (`ofprotocol`), a library for conversion from/to OpenFlow 1.3 (`oflib`), and a configuration tool (`dpctl`). This project is supported by Ericsson Innovation Center in Brazil and maintained by CPqD in technical collaboration with Ericsson Research.

OpenFlow laboratory with Mininet

Mininet is a software tool, which allows an entire OpenFlow network to be emulated on a single computer. Mininet uses lightweight process-based virtualization (Linux network namespaces and Linux container architecture) to run many hosts and switches (for instance 4096) on a single OS kernel. It can create kernel or user-space OpenFlow switches, controllers to control the switches, and hosts to communicate over the emulated network. Mininet connects switches and hosts using **virtual Ethernet (veth)** pairs. It considerably simplifies the initial development, debugging, testing, and deployment process. New network applications can be first developed and tested on an emulation of the anticipated deployment network. It can be then moved to the actual operational infrastructure. By default, Mininet supports OpenFlow v1.0. However, it may be modified to support a software switch that implements a newer release. Some of the key features and benefits of Mininet are as follows:

- Mininet creates a network of virtual hosts, switches, controllers, and links.
- Mininet hosts run standard Linux network software, and its switches support OpenFlow. It can be considered as an inexpensive OpenFlow laboratory for developing OpenFlow applications. It enables complex topology testing, without the need to wire up a physical network.

- Mininet includes a **command-line interface** (**CLI**) that is topology-aware and OpenFlow-aware, for debugging or running network-wide tests.
- You can start using Mininet out of the box without any programming, but it also provides a straightforward and extensible Python API for network creation and experimentation.
- Instead of being a simulation tool, Mininet is an emulation environment, which runs real, unmodified code, including application code, OS kernel code, and control plane code (both OpenFlow controller code and Open vSwitch code).
- It is easy to install and is available as a pre-packaged **virtual machine** (**VM**) image that runs on VMware or VirtualBox for Mac/Windows/Linux with OpenFlow v1.0 tools already installed.

In the rest of this section, we will provide a tutorial overview of Mininet, which will also be used in the rest of this book.

Getting started with Mininet

The easiest way of getting started with Mininet is to download a pre-packaged VM image of Mininet (which runs over Ubuntu). This VM includes all OpenFlow binaries, pre-installed tools to support large Mininet networks, along with Mininet itself. In addition to pre-packaged VM installation, interested readers can install it natively from source code or packages on Ubuntu.

The examples in this chapter are based on Version 2.0 of Mininet. The latest version of Mininet can be downloaded from: `www.mininet.org/download`.

In case you want to get the VM image, you have to download and install a virtualization system. VirtualBox (free, GPL) or VMwarePlayer (free for non-commercial use) are the available choices, which are free and work on Windows, OS X, and Linux. Mininet is an Open Virtualization Format (OVF) image file (approximately 1 GB), which can be imported by VirtualBox or VMware Player (free for non-commercial use). In VirtualBox, you can import the Mininet's OVF file by double-clicking on the VM image or go to **File** and select **Import Appliance**. Then go to **Settings** and add an additional *host-only network adapter* to log in to the VM image. If you are using VMware, it may ask you to install VMware tools on the VM; if it asks, decline. In the following examples, we have used VMware Player as our virtualization system for Mininet.

To reach the same environment, you can take the following steps:

- Start the Mininet VM image up in the virtualization program of your choice (VMware Player is shown in the following screenshot).
- Log in to the Mininet VM using the default username and password. The default username and password are both `mininet`. The root account is not enabled for login and you can use `sudo` to execute a command with superuser privileges.
- In order to establish an SSH session to the Mininet VM, you have to find the IP address of the VM. This address for VMware Player is probably in the range of `192.168.x.y`. Type the following command in the VM console:

  ```
  $ /sbin/ifocnfig eth0
  ```

- If you are using VirtualBox, and have set up a host-only network on eth1, you should use `$ /sbin/ifconfig eth1 eth1` instead.
- Assuming that VM is running locally, and that the additional precautions of `ssh -X` are not necessary, you can SSH to the VM using the `ssh -Y mininet@192.168.44.128` command, which has no authentication timeout by default. You have to change the IP address with the one that you get as the output of `ifconfig` command. Our setup in this section includes the Mininet VM over VMware Player, putty as our SSH client (with X-11 forwarding option enabled), and Xming X-Server. The X-11 forwarding (see the following information box for more information) enables you to execute programs with graphical output (for example, Wireshark, which is pre-installed and included in the Mininet VM image). In the following screenshot you can see the experimental environment based on VMware Player, Mininet, XMing (X-Server), and putty (SSH terminal).

- In the following screenshot, you can see that we have logged in to the Mininet VM using putty (SSH client) and then we have started the Wireshark as a background process (that is, `sudo wireshark &`). Since the X-11 forwarding is enabled, the Wireshark GUI appears as a separate window.

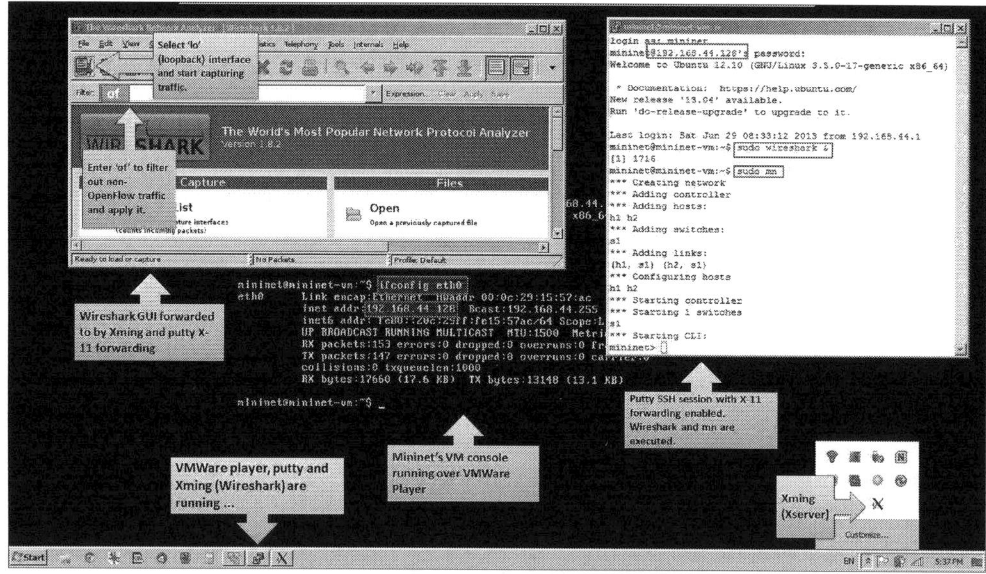

OpenFlow laboratory using Mininet.

- Before starting the Mininet emulator, you have to select the **Capture** device in Wireshark (lo or loopback interface) and start capturing the traffic. In order to display the OpenFlow related traffic, you have to add `of` (OpenFlow) in the filter box of Wireshark and apply it to the capturing traffic. This will instruct Wireshark to just display OpenFlow related traffic. Since Mininet is not started, no OpenFlow packets should be displayed in the main window of Wireshark. In the next section you will run a sample experiment using Mininet.

The Mininet VM does not include a desktop manager. The graphic output should be forwarded via X forwarding through SSH. You can consult the following FAQ to enable X11 forwarding. Setting X11 up correctly will enable you to run other GUI programs and the xterm terminal emulator, used later in this chapter. `https://github.com/mininet/mininet/wiki/FAQ#wiki-x11-forwarding`

Experimenting with Mininet

Mininet enables you to quickly create, customize, interact with, and share an OpenFlow prototype. Mininet's command line can be used to create a network (hosts and switches). Its CLI allows you to control and manage your entire virtual network from a single console. Furthermore, Mininet's API allows you to develop custom network applications with a few lines of Python script. Once a prototype works on Mininet, it can be deployed on a real-network.

In this sample experiment, we will use the default topology of Mininet (by running `$ sudo mn`). This topology includes one OpenFlow switch connected to two hosts, plus the OpenFlow reference controller. This topology could also be specified on the command line with `--topo=minimal`. Other topologies are also available out of the box in Mininet; see the `--topo` section in the output of `mn -h`. You can display nodes, links, and dump information about all nodes in the setup using the following commands respectively.

```
mininet> nodes
mininet> net
mininet> dump
```

Upon execution of Mininet emulation environment with default topology, the OpenFlow controller and switch initiate the OpenFlow protocol, which can be captured and viewed in the Wireshark capturing window. The following screenshot shows the captured traffic, which shows the `Hello` message, feature request/reply and several packet-in messages. This confirms that the OpenFlow switch in this setup is connected to the OpenFlow controller.

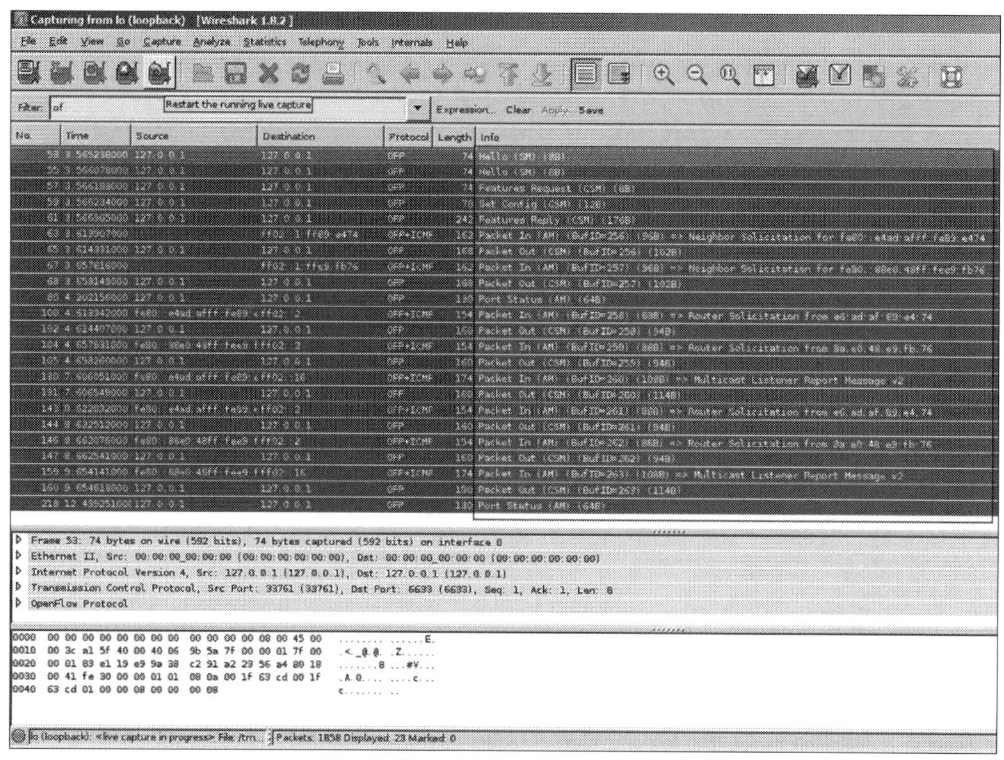

OpenFlow traffic, which is captured in Wireshark.

If the first string typed into the Mininet CLI (`mininet>`) is a host, switch, or controller name, the command is executed on that node. For example, you can see the Ethernet and loopback interface of first host (`h1`) using the following command:

```
mininet> h1 ifconfig -a
```

Now we can check the connectivity of each host by a simple ping command:

```
mininet> h1 ping -c 1 h2
```

This commands sends a single ping packet from `h1` to `h2`. The first host (h1) ARPs for the MAC address of the second (`h2`) causes a `packet_in` message to go to the OpenFlow controller. The controller then sends a `packet_out` message to flood the broadcast packet to other ports on the switch (in this example, the only other data port). The second host observes the ARP request and sends a broadcast reply. This reply goes to the controller, which sends it to the first host and pushes down a flow entry to the flow table of `s1` (OpenFlow switch).

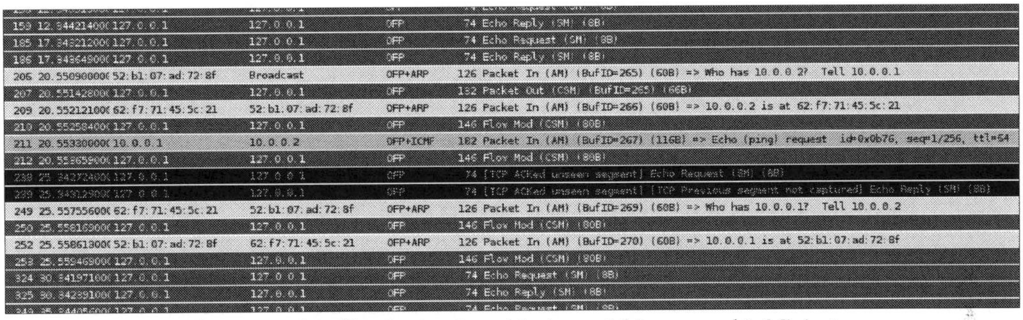

The captured traffic after issuing a h1 ping –c 1 h2command in Mininet.

Now the first host knows the IP address of the second, and can send its ping via an ICMP echo request. This request and its corresponding reply from the second host both go to the controller and results in a flow entry pushed down. The actual packets are getting sent out too. In our setup, the reported ping time is 3.93ms. We repeat the same ping command one more time:

```
mininet> h1 ping -c 1 h2
```

The ping time for the second ping command is decreased to just 0.25ms. A flow entry covering ICMP ping traffic was previously installed in the switch, so no control traffic was generated, and the packets immediately pass through the switch. An easier way to run this test is to use the Mininet CLI built-in `pingall` command, which does an all-pairs ping. Another useful test is a self-contained regression test. The following command created a minimal topology, started up the OpenFlow reference controller, ran an all-pairs-ping test, and tore down both the topology and the controller.

```
$ sudo mn --test pingpair
```

Another useful test is the performance evaluation using `iperf`.

```
$ sudo mn --test iperf
```

This commands needs a few seconds to complete. It creates the same Mininet topology (one controller, one switch, and two hosts), runs an `iperf` server on one host, an `iperf` client on the second host, and reports the TCP bandwidth between these two hosts.

Using Mininet's Python API, it is possible to define custom topologies for experiments. A built-in example is provided in `~/mininet/custom/topo-2sw-2host.py`. This example connects two switches directly, with a single host connected to each switch:

```
"""Custom topology example
Two directly connected switches plus a host for each switch:
   host --- switch --- switch --- host
  h1 <-> s3 <-> s4 <-> h2
Adding the 'topos' dict with a key/value pair to generate our newly
defined
topology enables one to pass in '--topo=mytopo' from the command line.
"""
from mininet.topo import Topo
class MyTopo( Topo ):
    "Simple topology example."
    def __init__( self ):
        "Create custom topo."
        # Initialize topology
        Topo.__init__( self )
        # Add hosts and switches
        leftHost = self.addHost( 'h1' )
        rightHost = self.addHost( 'h2' )
        leftSwitch = self.addSwitch( 's3' )
        rightSwitch = self.addSwitch( 's4' )
        # Add links
        self.addLink( leftHost, leftSwitch )
        self.addLink( leftSwitch, rightSwitch )
        self.addLink( rightSwitch, rightHost )
topos = { 'mytopo': ( lambda: MyTopo() ) }
```

Downloading the example code

You can download the example code files for all Packt books you have purchased from your account at http://www.packtpub.com. If you purchased this book elsewhere, you can visit http://www.packtpub.com/supportand register to have the files e-mailed directly to you.

This Python script can be passed as a command-line parameter to the Mininet. When a custom Mininet file is provided, it can add new topologies, switch types, and tests to the command line. For instance a `pingall` test can be executed using the mentioned topology with the following invocation of Mininet:

```
$ sudo mn --custom ~/mininet/custom/topo-2sw-2host.py --topo mytopo
--test pingall
```

For more complex debugging and also having access to the console of hosts, switch(es) or controller(s), you can start Mininet with `-x` command line parameter (that is, `sudo mn -x`). The xterms, which will pop up, are useful for running interactive commands. For instance in the xterm labeled, switch: s1 (root), you can run:

```
# dpctl dump-flows tcp:127.0.0.1:6634
```

Since the flow table of the switch s1 is empty, nothing will print out. Now in the xterm of host 1 (h1), you can ping the other host (h2) using normal ping command (# `ping 10.0.0.2`). If you go back to the xterm of switch s1, and dump the flow table, you should see multiple flow entries now. You can also use the `dpctl` built-in command in Mininet.

This was just a brief introduction to Mininet. In the following chapters we will use Mininet as part of our setup for experimenting with OpenFlow controllers and development of network applications. Interested readers can find more details on the Mininet web site: `www.mininet.org`.

Summary

The reference implementation of the OpenFlow switch includes `ofdatapath`, which implements the flow table in user space; `ofprotocol`, a program that implements the secure channel component of the reference switch; and `dpctl`, which is a tool for configuring the switch. There are three main message types in OpenFlow protocol (controller-to-switch, asynchronous, and symmetric messages). In addition to hardware OpenFlow switches, there is software implementation of OpenFlow in the form of soft-switches. Mininet is a network emulator, which runs a collection of end-hosts, switches, and links on a single Linux kernel. In this chapter we presented and used Mininet as an OpenFlow laboratory on a single computer. In the next chapter of this book, we will go through different SDN/OpenFlow controller options.

3

The OpenFlow Controllers

This chapter covers the role of the OpenFlow controllers, the interface to the switch, and the provided API for **Network Applications** (**Net Apps**). We will also see:

- The overall functionality of the OpenFlow (SDN) controllers
- The existing implementations (including NOX/POX, NodeFlow, Floodlight, and OpenDaylight)
- Special controllers or applications over controllers (FlowVisor and RouteFlow)

SDN controllers

The decoupled control and data plane architecture of **software-defined networking** (**SDN**), as depicted in the following figure, and in particular OpenFlow can be compared with an operating system and computer hardware. The OpenFlow controller (similar to the operating system) provides a programmatic interface to the OpenFlow switches (similar to the computer hardware). Using this programmatic interface, network applications, referred to as Net Apps, can be written to perform control and management tasks and offer new functionalities. The control plane in SDN and OpenFlow in particular is logically centralized and Net Apps are written as if the network is a single system.

With a *reactive* control model, the OpenFlow switches must consult an OpenFlow controller each time a decision must be made, such as when a new packet flow reaches an OpenFlow switch (that is, `Packet_in` event). In the case of flow-based control granularity, there will be a small performance delay as the first packet of each new flow is forwarded to the controller for decision (for example, forward or drop), after which future traffic within that flow will be forwarded at line rate within the switching hardware. While the first-packet delay is negligible in many cases, it may be a concern if the central OpenFlow controller is geographically remote or if most flows are short-lived (for example, as single-packet flows). An alternative *proactive* approach is also possible in OpenFlow to push policy rules out from the controller to the switches.

While this simplifies the control, management, and policy enforcement tasks, the bindings must be closely maintained between the controller and OpenFlow switches. The first important concern of this centralized control is the scalability of the system and the second one is the placement of controllers. A recent study of the several OpenFlow controller implementations (NOX-MT, Maestro, and Beacon), conducted on a large emulated network with 100,000 hosts and up to 256 switches, revealed that all OpenFlow controllers were able to handle at least 50,000 new flow requests per second in each of the experimental scenarios. Furthermore, new OpenFlow controllers under development, such as Mc-Nettle (`http://haskell.cs.yale.edu/nettle/mcnettle/`) target powerful multicore servers and are being designed to scale up to large data center workloads (for example, 20 million flow requests per second and up to 5,000 switches). In packet switching networks, traditionally, each packet contains the required information for a network switch to make individual routing decisions. However, most applications send data as a flow of many individual packets. The control granularity in OpenFlow is in the scale of flows, not packets. When controlling individual flows, the decision made for the first packet of the flow can be applied to all the subsequent packets of the flow within the data plane (OpenFlow switches). The overhead may be further reduced by grouping the flows together, such as all traffic between two hosts, and performing control decisions on the aggregated flows.

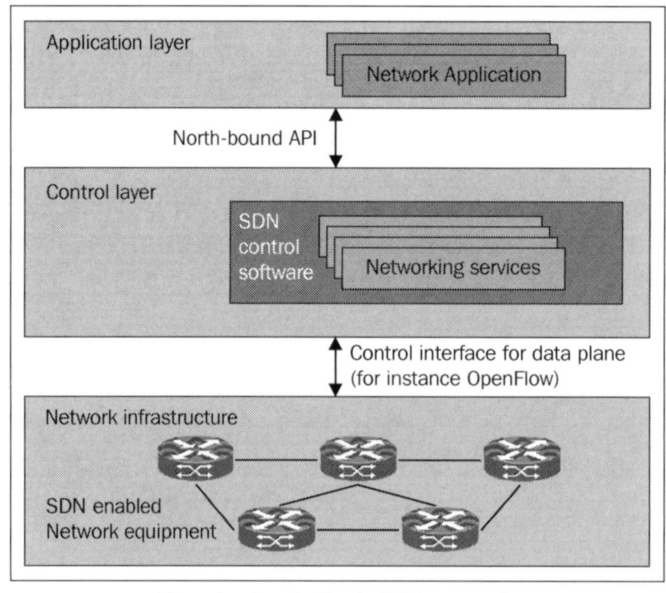

The role of controller in SDN approach

Multiple controllers may be used to reduce the latency or increase the scalability and fault tolerance of the OpenFlow (SDN) deployment. OpenFlow allows the connection of multiple controllers to a switch, which would allow backup controllers to take over in the event of a failure. Onix and HyperFlow take the idea further by attempting to maintain a logically centralized, but physically distributed control plane. This decreases the lookup overhead by enabling communication with local controllers, while still allowing applications to be written with a simplified central view of the network. The potential main downside of this approach is maintaining the consistent state in the overall distributed system. This may cause Net Apps, that believe they have an accurate view of the network, to act incorrectly due to inconsistency in the global network state.

Recalling the operating system analogy, an OpenFlow controller acts as a network operating system and should implement at least two interfaces: a *southbound* interface that allows OpenFlow switches to communicate with the controller, and a *northbound* interface that presents a programmable application programming interface (API) to network control and management applications (that is, Net Apps). The existing southbound interface is OpenFlow protocol (covered in *Chapter 2, Implementing the OpenFlow Switch*) as an early SDN southbound interface implementation. External control and management systems/software or network services may wish to extract information about the underlying network or enforce policies, or control an aspect of the network behavior. Besides, a primary OpenFlow controller may need to share policy information with a backup controller, or to communicate with other controllers across multiple control domains. While the southbound interface (for example, OpenFlow or ForCES, `http://datatracker.ietf.org/wg/forces/charter/`) is well defined and can be considered as a de facto standard, there is no widely accepted standard for northbound interactions, and they are more likely to be implemented on a use-case basis for particular applications.

Existing implementations

Currently, there are different OpenFlow (and SDN) controller implementations, which we will introduce in more detail in *Chapter 8, Open Source Resources*, as part of existing open source projects. In this chapter, we limit ourselves to NOX, POX, NodeFlow, Floodlight (which is forked from Beacon), and OpenDaylight to present some OpenFlow controllers and different possibilities for choosing a programming language to develop the network applications.

NOX and POX

NOX (`www.noxrepo.org`) was the first OpenFlow controller written in C++ and provides API for Python too. It has been the basis for many research and development projects in the early exploration of OpenFlow and SDN space. NOX has two separate lines of development:

- NOX-Classic
- NOX, also known as new NOX

The former is the well-known line of development, which contains support for Python and C++ along with a bunch of network applications. However, this line of development is deprecated and there is no plan for further development on NOX-Classic. New NOX only supports C++. It has fewer network applications compared to NOX-Classic, but is much faster and has a much cleaner codebase. POX is Python-only version of NOX. It can be considered as a general, open source OpenFlow controller written in Python, and a platform for rapid development and prototyping of network applications. The primary target of POX is research. Since many of the research projects are short-lived by nature, the focus of the developers of POX is on right interfaces rather than maintaining a stable API. NOX (and POX) are managed in Git source code repositories on GitHub. Cloning the Git repository is the preferred way to get NOX and POX. POX branches fall into two categories: active and released. Active branches are branches that are being actively developed. Released branches are branches, which at some point were selected as being a new version. The most recently released branch may continue to get worked on, but only in the form of bug fixes—new features always go into the active branch. You can get the latest version of NOX and POX with the following commands:

```
$ git clone http://noxrepo.org/git/nox
$ git clone http://www.github.com/noxrepo/pox
```

In *Chapter 2, Implementing the OpenFlow Switch*, we set up the OpenFlow laboratory using Mininet emulation environment. In this section, we start with a Net App, which behaves as a simple Ethernet hub. You can change it to a learning Ethernet L2 switch as a homework. In this application, the switch will examine each packet and learn the source-port mapping. Thereafter, the source MAC address will be associated with the port. If the destination of the packet is already associated with some port, the packet will be sent to the given port, else it will be flooded on all ports of the switch. The first step is to start your OpenFlow VM. Then you need to download the POX into your VM:

```
$ git clone http://github.com/noxrepo/pox
$ cd pox
```

Running a POX application

After getting the POX controller, you can try running a basic hub example in POX as follows:

```
$./pox.py log.level --DEBUG misc.of_tutorial
```

This command line tells POX to enable verbose logging and to start the of_tutorial component, which you will be using. This of_tutorial component acts as an Ethernet hub. Now you can start the Mininet OpenFlow laboratory using the following command line:

```
$ sudo mn --topo single,3 --mac --switch ovsk --controller remote
```

The switches may take a little bit of time to connect. When an OpenFlow switch loses its connection to a controller, it will generally increase the period between which it attempts to contact the controller, up to a maximum of 15 seconds. This timer is implementation specific and can be defined by the user. Since the OpenFlow switch has not connected yet, this delay may be anything between 0 and 15 seconds. If this is too long to wait, the switch can be configured to wait no more than `N` seconds using the `--max-backoff` parameter. Wait until the application indicates that the OpenFlow switch has connected. When the switch connects, POX will print something like the following:

```
INFO:openflow.of_01:[Con 1/1] Connected to 00-00-00-00-00-01
DEBUG:samples.of_tutorial:Controlling [Con 1/1]
```

The first line is from the portion of POX that handles OpenFlow connections. The second line is from the tutorial component itself.

Now, we verify that the hosts can ping each other, and that all the hosts see the exact same traffic: the behavior of a hub. To do this, we will create xterms for each host and view the traffic in each. In the Mininet console, start up three xterms:

```
mininet> xterm h1 h2 h3
```

Arrange each xterm so that they're all on the screen at once. This may require reducing the height to fit on a cramped laptop screen. In the xterms for `h2` and `h3`, run `tcpdump`, a utility to print the packets seen by a host:

```
# tcpdump -XX -n -i h2-eth0
```

And respectively:

```
# tcpdump -XX -n -i h3-eth0
```

In the xterm for `h1`, issue a ping command:

```
# ping -c1 10.0.0.2
```

The ping packets are now going up to the controller, which then floods them out of all interfaces except the sending one. You should see identical ARP and ICMP packets corresponding to the ping in both xterms running `tcpdump`. This is how a hub works; it sends all packets to every port on the network. Now, see what happens when a non-existent host doesn't reply. From `h1` xterm:

```
# ping -c1 10.0.0.5
```

You should see three unanswered ARP requests in the `tcpdump` xterms. If your code is off later, three unanswered ARP requests is a signal that you might be accidentally dropping packets. You can close the xterms now.

In order to change the behavior of the hub to a learning switch, you have to add the learning switch functionality to `of_tutorial.py`. Go to your SSH terminal and stop the tutorial hub controller by pressing *Ctrl* + *C*. The file you'll modify is `pox/misc/of_tutorial.py`. Open `pox/misc/of_tutorial.py` in your favorite editor. The current code calls `act_like_hub()` from the handler for `packet_in` messages to implement the switch behavior. You will want to switch to using the `act_like_switch()` function, which contains a sketch of what your final learning switch code should look like. Each time you change and save this file, make sure to restart POX, then use pings to verify the behavior of the combination of switch and controller as a:

1. Hub.
2. Controller-based Ethernet learning switch.
3. Flow-accelerated learning switch.

For 2 and 3, hosts that are not the destination for a ping should display no `tcpdump` traffic after the initial broadcast ARP request. Python is a dynamic and interpreted language. There is no separate compilation step, just update your code and re-run it. Python has built-in hash tables, called dictionaries, and vectors, called lists. Some of the common operations that you need for learning switch are as follows:

- To initialize a dictionary:

  ```
  mactable = {}
  ```

- To add an element to a dictionary:

  ```
  mactable[0x123] = 2
  ```

- To check for dictionary membership:

```
if 0x123 in mactable:
    print 'element 2 is in mactable'
if 0x123 not in mactable:
    print 'element 2 is not in mactable'
```

- To print a debug message in POX:

```
log.debug('saw new MAC!')
```

- To print an error message in POX:

```
log.error('unexpected packet causing system meltdown!')
```

- To print all member variables and functions of an object:

```
print dir(object)
```

- To comment a line of code:

```
# Prepend comments with a #; no // or /**/
```

You can find more Python resources at the following URLs.
List of built-in functions in Python:
`http://docs.python.org/2/library/functions.html`
Official Python tutorial:
`http://docs.python.org/2/tutorial/`

In addition to the preceding mentioned functions, you also need some details about the POX APIs, which are useful for the development of learning switch. There is also other documentation available in the appropriate section of POX's website.

Sending OpenFlow messages with POX:

```
connection.send( ... ) # send an OpenFlow message to a switch
```

When a connection to a switch starts, a `ConnectionUp` event is fired. The example code creates a new `Tutorial` object that holds a reference to the associated `Connection` object. This can later be used to send commands (OpenFlow messages) to the switch:

```
ofp_action_output class
```

This is an action for use with `ofp_packet_out` and `ofp_flow_mod`. It specifies a switch port that you wish to send the packet out of. It can also take various special port numbers. An example of this would be `OFPP_FLOOD`, which sends the packet out on all ports except the one the packet originally arrived on. The following example creates an output action that would send packets to all ports:

```
out_action = of.ofp_action_output(port = of.OFPP_FLOOD)
ofp_match class
```

Objects of this class describe packet header fields and an input port to match on. All fields are optional, items that are not specified are wildcards, and will match on anything. Some notable fields of `ofp_match` objects are:

- `dl_src`: The data link layer (MAC) source address
- `dl_dst`: The data link layer (MAC) destination address
- `in_port`: The packet input switch port

Example: Create a match that matches packets arriving on port 3:

```
match = of.ofp_match()
match.in_port = 3
ofp_packet_out OpenFlow message
```

The `ofp_packet_out` message instructs a switch to send a packet. The packet might be constructed at the controller, or it might be the one that the switch received, buffered, and forwarded to the controller (and is now referenced by a `buffer_id`). Notable fields are:

- `buffer_id`: The `buffer_id` of a buffer you wish to send. Do not set if you are sending a constructed packet.
- `data`: Raw bytes you wish the switch to send. Do not set if you are sending a buffered packet.
- `actions`: A list of actions to apply (for this tutorial, this is just a single `ofp_action_output action`).
- `in_port`: The port number this packet initially arrived on, if you are sending by `buffer_id`, otherwise `OFPP_NONE`.

Example: The `send_packet()` method `of_tutorial`:

```
def send_packet (self, buffer_id, raw_data, out_port, in_port):
  """
  Sends a packet out of the specified switch port.
  If buffer_id is a valid buffer on the switch, use that.
  Otherwise, send the raw data in raw_data.
```

```
    The "in_port" is the port number that packet arrived on.  Use
    OFPP_NONE if you're generating this packet.
    """
    msg = of.ofp_packet_out()
    msg.in_port = in_port
    if buffer_id != -1 and buffer_id is not None:
      # We got a buffer ID from the switch; use that
      msg.buffer_id = buffer_id
    else:
      # No buffer ID from switch -- we got the raw data
      if raw_data is None:
        # No raw_data specified -- nothing to send!
        return
      msg.data = raw_data

    action = of.ofp_action_output(port = out_port)
    msg.actions.append(action)

    # Send message to switch
    self.connection.send(msg)
  ofp_flow_mod OpenFlow message
```

This instructs a switch to install a flow table entry. Flow table entries match some fields of the incoming packets, and execute a list of actions on the matching packets. The actions are the same as for `ofp_packet_out`, mentioned previously (and again, for the tutorial all you need is the simple `ofp_action_output` action). The match is described by an `ofp_match` object. Notable fields are:

- `idle_timeout`: Number of idle seconds before the flow entry is removed. Defaults to no idle timeout.
- `hard_timeout`: Number of seconds before the flow entry is removed. Defaults to no timeout.
- `actions`: A list of actions to be performed on matching packets (for example, `ofp_action_output`).
- `priority`: When using non-exact (wildcarded) matches, this specifies the priority for overlapping matches. Higher values have higher priority. Not important for exact or non-overlapping entries.
- `buffer_id`: The `buffer_id` field of a buffer to apply the actions to immediately. Leave unspecified for none.

- `in_port`: If using a `buffer_id`, this is the associated input port.
- `match`: An `ofp_match` object. By default, this matches everything, so you should probably set some of its fields.

Example: Create `flow_mod`, that sends packets from port `3` out of port `4`:

```
fm = of.ofp_flow_mod()
fm.match.in_port = 3
fm.actions.append(of.ofp_action_output(port = 4))
```

For more information about OpenFlow constants, see the main OpenFlow `types/enums/structs` file, `openflow.h`, in `~/openflow/include/openflow/openflow.h` You may also wish to consult POX's OpenFlow library in `pox/openflow/libopenflow_01.py`, and, of course, the OpenFlow 1.0 specification.

The POX packet library is used to parse packets and make each protocol field available to Python. This library can also be used to construct packets for sending. The parsing libraries are present in `pox/lib/packet/`.

Each protocol has a corresponding parsing file. For the first exercise, you'll only need to access the Ethernet source and destination fields. To extract the source of a packet, use the dot notation:

```
packet.src
```

The Ethernet `src` and `dst` fields are stored as `pox.lib.addresses.EthAddr` objects. These can easily be converted to their common string representation (`str(addr)` will return something like `"01:ea:be:02:05:01"`), or created from their common string representation (`EthAddr("01:ea:be:02:05:01")`). To see all members of a parsed packet object:

```
print dir(packet)
```

Here's what you'd see for an ARP packet:

```
['HW_TYPE_ETHERNET', 'MIN_LEN', 'PROTO_TYPE_IP', 'REPLY', 'REQUEST',
'REV_REPLY',
 'REV_REQUEST', '__class__', '__delattr__', '__dict__', '__doc__',
'__format__',
 '__getattribute__', '__hash__', '__init__', '__len__', '__module__',
'__new__',
 '__nonzero__', '__reduce__', '__reduce_ex__', '__repr__', '__
setattr__',
 '__sizeof__', '__str__', '__subclasshook__', '__weakref__', '_init',
'err',
```

```
 'find', 'hdr', 'hwdst', 'hwlen', 'hwsrc', 'hwtype', 'msg', 'next',
'opcode',
 'pack', 'parse', 'parsed', 'payload', 'pre_hdr', 'prev', 'protodst',
'protolen',
 'protosrc', 'prototype', 'raw', 'set_payload', 'unpack', 'warn']
```

Many fields are common to all the Python objects and can be ignored, but this can be a quick way to avoid a trip to a function's documentation.

NodeFlow

NodeFlow (`http://garyberger.net/?p=537`, developed by *Gary Berger*, Technical Leader, Office of the CTO of Cisco Systems) is a minimalist OpenFlow controller written in JavaScript for Node.js (`www.nodejs.org`). Node.js is a server-side software system designed for writing scalable Internet applications (for example, HTTP servers). It can be considered as a packaged compilation of Google's V8 JavaScript engine, the *libuv* platform abstraction layer, and a core library, which is written in JavaScript. Node.js uses an event-driven, non-blocking I/O model that makes it lightweight and efficient, perfect for data-intensive real-time applications that run across distributed devices. Programs are written on the server side in JavaScript, using event-driven, asynchronous I/O to minimize overhead and maximize the scalability. Therefore, unlike most JavaScript programs, the program is not executed in a web browser. Instead, it runs as a server-side JavaScript application. NodeFlow is actually a very simple program and relies heavily on a protocol interpreter called OFLIB-NODE written by *Zoltan LaJos Kis*. NodeFlow is an experimental system available at GitHub (`git://github.com/gaberger/NodeFLow`) along with a fork of the OFLIB-NODE libraries (`git://github.com/gaberger/oflib-node`). The beauty of NodeFlow is its simplicity on running and understanding an OpenFlow controller with less than 500 lines of code. Leveraging JavaScript and the high performance Google's V8 JavaScript engine allows for network architects to experiment with various SDN features without the need to deal with all of the boilerplate code required for setting up event driven programming.

The NodeFlow server (that is, OpenFlow controller) instantiates with a simple call to `net.createServer`. The address and listening port are configured through a start script:

```
NodeFlowServer.prototype.start = function(address, port) {
var self = this
var socket = []
var server = net.createServer()
server.listen(port, address, function(err, result) {
util.log("NodeFlow listening on:" + address + '@' + port)
self.emit('started', { "Config": server.address() })
})
```

The next step is to create a unique session ID, from which the controller can keep track of each of the different switch connections. The event listener maintains the socket. The main event processing loop is invoked whenever data is received from the socket channel. The stream library is utilized to buffer the data and return the decoded OpenFlow message in `msgs` object. The `msgs` object is passed to the `_ProcessMessage` function for further processing:

```
server.on('connection',
  function(socket) {
    socket.setNoDelay(noDelay = true)
    var sessionID = socket.remoteAddress + ":" + socket.remotePort
    sessions[sessionID] = new sessionKeeper(socket)
    util.log("Connection from : " + sessionID)

    socket.on('data', function(data) {
    var msgs = switchStream.process(data);
    msgs.forEach(function(msg) {
    if (msg.hasOwnProperty('message')) {
         self._processMessage(msg, sessionID)
    } else {
         util.log('Error: Cannot parse the message.')
         console.dir(data)
   }
})
```

The last part is the event handlers. `EventEmitters` of Node.js is utilized to trigger the callbacks. These event handlers wait for the specific event to happen and then trigger the processing. NodeFlow handles two specific events: `OFPT_PACKET_IN`, which is the main event to listen on for OpenFlow `PACKET_IN` events, and `SENDPACKET`, which simply encodes and sends out OpenFlow messages:

```
self.on('OFPT_PACKET_IN',
  function(obj) {
  var packet = decode.decodeethernet(obj.message.body.data, 0)
  nfutils.do_l2_learning(obj, packet)
  self._forward_l2_packet(obj, packet)
  })
  self.on('SENDPACKET',
  function(obj) {
  nfutils.sendPacket(obj.type, obj.packet.outmessage,
  obj.packet.sessionID)
  })
```

The simple Net App based on NodeFlow could be a learning switch (following `do_l2_learning` function). The learning switch simply searches for the source MAC address and in case the address is not already in the learning table, it will be inserted in the corresponding source port to the forwarding table:

```
do_l2_learning: function(obj, packet) {
  self = this
  var dl_src = packet.shost
  var dl_dst = packet.dhost
  var in_port = obj.message.body.in_port
  var dpid = obj.dpid
  if (dl_src == 'ff:ff:ff:ff:ff:ff') {
  return
  }
if (!l2table.hasOwnProperty(dpid)) {
  l2table[dpid] = new Object() //create object
  }
if (l2table[dpid].hasOwnProperty(dl_src)) {
  var dst = l2table[dpid][dl_src]
     if (dst != in_port) {
       util.log("MAC has moved from " + dst + " to " + in_port)
     } else {
          return
     }
} else {
     util.log("learned mac " + dl_src + " port : " + in_port)
     l2table[dpid][dl_src] = in_port
}
  if (debug) {
     console.dir(l2table)
 }
}
```

The complete NodeFlow server is called `server.js`, which can be downloaded from NodeFlow Git repository. To run the NodeFlow controller, execute the Node.js and pass the NodeFlow server (that is, `server.js`) to the `Node.js` binary (for example, `node.exe` on Windows):

```
C:\ program Files\nodejs>node server.js
```

Floodlight

Floodlight is a Java-based OpenFlow controller, based on the Beacon implementation, which supports both physical and virtual OpenFlow switches. Beacon is a cross platform, modular OpenFlow controller, also implemented in Java. It supports event-based and threaded operation. Beacon was created by *David Erickson* at Stanford University as a Java-based, and cross platform OpenFlow controller. Prior to being licensed under GPL v2, Floodlight was forked from Beacon, which carries on with an Apache license. Floodlight has been redesigned without the OSGI framework. Therefore, it can be built, run, and modified without OSGI experience. Besides, Floodlight's community currently includes a number of developers at Big Switch Networks who are actively testing and fixing bugs, and building additional tools, plugins, and features for it. The Floodlight controller is intended to be a platform for a wide variety of network applications (Net Apps). Net Apps are important, since they provide solutions to real-world networking problems. Some of the Floodlight's Net Apps are:

- The Virtual Networking Filter, which identifies packets that enter the network, but do not match an existing flow. The application determines whether the source and destination are on the same virtual network; if so, the application signals the controller to continue the flow creation. This filter is in fact a simple layer 2 (MAC) based network virtualization, which enables users to create multiple logical layer 2 networks in a single layer 2 domain.
- The Static Flow Pusher is used to create a flow in advance of the initial packet in the flow that enters the network. It is exposed via Floodlight's REST API that allows a user to manually insert flows into an OpenFlow network.
- The Circuit Pusher creates a flow and provisions switches along the path to the packet's destination. The bidirectional circuit between source and destination is a permanent flow entry, on all switches in the route between the two devices.
- Firewall modules give the same protection to devices on the software-defined network as traditional firewalls on a physical network. **Access Control List** (**ACL**) rules control whether a flow should be set up to a specific destination. The Firewall application has been implemented as a Floodlight Module that enforces ACL rules on OpenFlow enabled switches in the network. The packet monitoring is done using the packet-in messages.

- Floodlight can be run as a network plugin for OpenStack using a Neutron. Neutron plugin exposes a **Networking-as-a-Service** (**NaaS**) model via a REST API that is implemented by Floodlight. This solution has two components: a VirtualNetworkFilter module in Floodlight (that implements the Neutron API) and the Neutron RestProxy plugin that connects Floodlight to Neutron. Once a Floodlight controller is integrated into OpenStack, network engineers can dynamically provision network resources alongside other virtual and physical computer resources. This improves the overall flexibility and performance.

For more details and tutorials see the FloodLight OpenFlowHub page, `http://www.projectfloodlight.org/floodlight/`.

OpenDaylight

OpenDaylight is a Linux Foundation Collaborative project (`www.opendaylight.org`), in which a community has come together to fill the need for an open and reference framework for programmability and control through an open source SDN solution. It combines open community developers, open source code, and project governance that guarantees an open, community decision-making process on business and technical issues. OpenDaylight can be a core component within any SDN architecture. Building upon an open source SDN controller enables users to reduce operational complexity, extend the lifetime of their existing network infrastructure, and enable new services and capabilities only available with SDN. The mission statement of OpenDaylight project can be read as "OpenDaylight facilitates a community-led industry-supported open source framework, including code and architecture, to accelerate and advance a common, robust Software-Defined Networking platform". OpenDaylight is open to anyone. Anyone can develop and contribute code, get elected to the Technical Steering Committee (TSC), get voted onto the Board, or help steer the project forward in any number of ways. OpenDaylight will be composed of numerous projects. Each project will have contributors, committers, and one committer elected by their peers to be the Project Lead. The initial TSC and project leads will be composed of the experts who developed the code that has been originally contributed to the project. This ensures that the community gets access to the experts most familiar with the contributed code to ramp up and provide mentorship to new community participants. Among initial bootstrap projects, OpenDaylight (ODL) controller is one of the early projects, which we will introduce in the next section, and then we set up our environment for ODL-based Net App development OpenDaylight is covered with more details in next chapter (*Chapter 4, Setting Up the Environment*).

Special controllers

In addition to the OpenFlow controllers that we introduced in this chapter, there are also two special purpose OpenFlow controllers: FlowVisor and RouteFlow. The former acts as a transparent proxy between OpenFlow switches and multiple OpenFlow controllers. It is able to create network slices and can delegate control of each slice to a different OpenFlow controller. FlowVisor also isolates these slices from each other by enforcing proper policies. RouteFlow, on the other hand, provides virtualized IP routing over OpenFlow capable hardware. RouteFlow can be considered as a network application on top of OpenFlow controllers. It is composed by an OpenFlow Controller application, an independent server, and a virtual network environment that reproduces the connectivity of a physical infrastructure and runs the IP routing engines. The routing engines generate the forwarding information base (FIB) into the Linux IP tables according to the configured routing protocols (for example, OSPF and BGP). These special controllers are presented in more detail in the further chapters. These controllers are covered in more details in *Chapter 8, Open Source Resources*.

Summary

The OpenFlow controller provides the interfaces to the OpenFlow switches on one side and provides the required API for the development of Net Apps (that is, Network Applications). In this chapter the overall functionality of OpenFlow (SDN) controllers were presented and some of the existing implementations (NOX/POX, NodeFlow, and Floodlight) were explained in more detail. NOX was the first OpenFlow controller written in Python and C++. POX is a general, open-source SDN controller written in Python. A learning Ethernet switch Net App, based on the API of POX was presented. NodeFlow is an OpenFlow controller written in JavaScript for Node.js. Floodlight is a Java-based OpenFlow controller, based on the Beacon implementation, that works with physical and virtual OpenFlow switches. FlowVisor and RouteFlow as special controllers were also presented in this chapter. Now, we have covered all the required material in order to set up our SDN/OpenFlow development environment. In the next chapter this environment will be set up.

4

Setting Up the Environment

In the previous chapters, we introduced the OpenFlow switch and controllers and in this chapter we will complete and set up the infrastructure and environment for Net App development. We start with our OpenFlow laboratory based on Mininet and remote OpenFlow controllers (POX), and then we introduce the OpenDaylight project and its bootstrap project ODL controller as an SDN controller platform (with OpenFlow support) that can be used for our Net App development.

Understanding the OpenFlow laboratory

In *Chapter 2, Implementing the OpenFlow Switch*, we introduced the Mininet network emulation platform as an OpenFlow laboratory. In this section, we present this laboratory in more detail as it is going to be part of our development environment. Mininet uses lightweight virtualization in the Linux kernel to make a single system look like a complete network. A Mininet host behaves just like a real machine; you can establish an SSH session into it (if you start up SSH daemon and bridge the network to your host) and run arbitrary programs (anything that runs on Linux is available for you to run, from web servers, to Wireshark, to iperf). However, Mininet uses a single Linux kernel for all virtual hosts; this means that you can't run software that depends on BSD, Windows, or other operating systems. Currently, Mininet does not support **Network Address Translation** (**NAT**) by default. This means that your virtual hosts will be isolated from your LAN by default. While this is usually a good thing, it means that your virtual hosts do not have access to the Internet. Furthermore, Mininet hosts (that is, virtual hosts) share the host file system and **process ID** (**PID**) space. This means that you have to be careful if you are running daemons that require configuration in `/etc`. You also need to be careful not to kill the wrong processes by mistake.

Mininet utilizes specific features built into Linux operating system that allow a single system to be split into a bunch of smaller "containers", each with a fixed share of the processing power, combined with a virtual link code that allows links (for example, Ethernet connections) with accurate delays and speeds (for example, 100 Mbps or 1 Gbps). Internally, Mininet employs lightweight virtualization features in the Linux kernel, including process groups, CPU bandwidth isolation, and network namespaces, and combines them with link schedulers and virtual Ethernet links.
A virtual host in Mininet is a group of user-level processes moved into a network namespace (a container for network state). Network namespaces provide process groups with exclusive ownership of interfaces, ports, and routing tables (such as, ARP and IP). The data rate of each emulated Ethernet link in Mininet is enforced by Linux **Traffic Control (tc)**, which has a number of packet schedulers to shape traffic to a configured rate. Mininet allows you to set link parameters, and these can even be set automatically from the command line:

```
$ sudo mn --link tc,bw=10,delay=10ms
mininet> iperf
...
mininet> h1 ping -c10 h2
```

This will set the bandwidth of the links to 10 Mbps and a delay of 10 ms. Given this delay value, the **round trip time** (**RTT**) should be about 40 ms, since the ICMP request traverses two links (one to the switch, one to the destination) and the ICMP reply traverses two links coming back.

[You can customize each link using the Python API of Mininet: `http://github.com/mininet/mininet/wiki/Introduction-to-Mininet`.]

Each virtual host has its own virtual Ethernet interface(s). A virtual Ethernet (or **veth**) pair, acts like a wire connecting two virtual interfaces, or virtual switch ports; packets sent through one interface are delivered to the other, and each interface appears as a fully functional Ethernet port to all system and application software. Mininet typically uses the default Linux bridge or Open vSwitch running in kernel mode to switch packets across the interfaces as shown in the following figure:

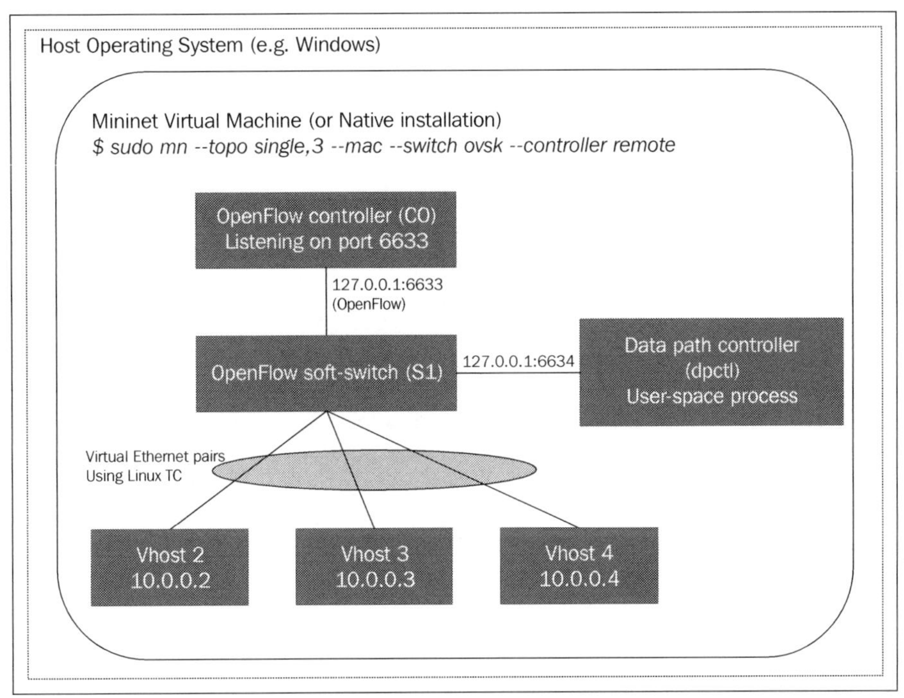

A sample experimental network inside the OpenFlow Laboratory

The preceding figure presents the virtual hosts, soft switch, and the OpenFlow controller, which are created inside the Mininet Linux server (or Mininet Linux VM image). To create this network topology, you can simply enter the following command in an SSH terminal:

```
$ sudo mn --topo single,3 --mac --switch ovsk --controller remote
```

This command line instructs Mininet to start up a 3-host, single-(Open vSwitch-based) switch topology (`--topo single,3`), set the MAC address of each host equal to its IP address (`--mac`), and point to a remote controller (`--controller remote`), which defaults to the localhost. Each virtual host has its own separate IP address. A single OpenFlow soft-switch in the kernel with 3 ports is also created. Virtual hosts are connected to the soft-switch with virtual Ethernet links. The MAC address of each host is set to its IP address. Finally, the OpenFlow soft-switch is connected to a remote controller.

The examples directory (`~/mininet/examples`) in the Mininet source tree includes examples of how to use Mininet's Python API, and potentially useful code that has not been integrated into the main code base of Mininet.

In addition to the mentioned components, `dpctl` is a utility that comes with the OpenFlow reference distribution and enables visibility and control over a single switch's flow table. It is especially useful for debugging purposes and to provide visibility over flow state and flow counters. To obtain this information you can poll the switch on port `6634`. The following command in an SSH window connects to the switch and dumps out its port state and capabilities:

```
$ dpctl show tcp:127.0.0.1:6634
```

The following command dumps the flow table of the soft-switch:

```
$ dpctl dump-flows tcp:127.0.0.1:6634
stats_reply (xid=0x1b5ffa1c): flags=none type=1(flow) cookie=0,
duration_sec=1538s, duration_nsec=567000000s, table_id=0,
priority=500, n_packets=0, n_bytes=0, idle_timeout=0,hard_timeout=0,in_
port=1,actions=output:2
  cookie=0, duration_sec=1538s, duration_nsec=567000000s, table_id=0,
priority=500, n_packets=0, n_bytes=0, idle_timeout=0,hard_timeout=0,in_
port=2,actions=output:1
```

You can also use `dpctl` to manually install the necessary flows. For example:

```
$ dpctl add-flow tcp:127.0.0.1:6634 in_port=1,actions=output:2
$ dpctl add-flow tcp:127.0.0.1:6634 in_port=2,actions=output:1
```

It will forward packets coming at port 1 to port 2 and vice-versa. This can be checked by dumping the flow table:

```
$ dpctl dump-flows tcp:127.0.0.1:6634
```

By default, Mininet runs Open vSwitch in OpenFlow mode, which requires an OpenFlow controller. Mininet comes with built-in `Controller()` classes to support several controllers, including the OpenFlow reference controller (controller), Open vSwitch's ovs-controller, and the now-deprecated NOX Classic. You can simply choose which OpenFlow controller you want when you invoke the `mn` command:

```
$ sudo mn --controller ref
$ sudo mn --controller ovsc
$ sudo mn --controller NOX,pyswitch
```

Each of these examples uses a controller which turns your OVS switch into an Ethernet learning switch.

ovsc is easy to install, but only supports 16 switches. You can install the reference controller using `install.sh -f`. You can also install NOX Classic using `install.sh -x`, but note that NOX Classic is deprecated and may not be supported in the future.

External controllers

When you start a Mininet network, each switch can be connected to a remote controller, which could be in the Mininet VM, outside the Mininet VM, and on your local machine, or in principle anywhere in the Internet. This setup may be convenient if you already have a controller framework and development tool installed on the local host or you want to test a controller running on a different physical machine. If you want to try this, you have to make sure that your controller is reachable from Mininet VM and fill in the host IP and (optionally) listening port:

```
$ sudo mn --controller=remote,ip=[controller IP],port=[controller listening port]
```

For instance, to run POX's sample learning switch, you could do something like:

```
$ cd ~/pox
$ ./pox.py forwarding.l2_learning
```

in one window, and in another window, start up Mininet to connect to the remote controller (which is actually running locally, but outside of Mininet's control):

```
$ sudo mn --controller=remote,ip=127.0.0.1,port=6633
```

Note that these are actually the default IP address and port values. If you generate some traffic (`mininet> h1 ping h2`) you should be able to observe some output in the POX window showing that the switch has connected and that some flow table entries have been installed.

Completing the OpenFlow laboratory

Our OpenFlow laboratory consists of four key building blocks:

- A virtualization software, for example, VirtualBox or VMware Player, to host the Mininet VM
- A terminal program with SSH support, for example, PuTTY
- An X Server for X11 forwarding, for example, Xming or XQuartz
- The Mininet (2.0) VM image

The following figure shows the complete building blocks and setup of the OpenFlow laboratory that will be used for Net App development. A number of OpenFlow (and SDN) controller frameworks are readily available and should work readily with Mininet as long as you start them up and specify the remote controller option with the correct IP address of the host, where your controller is located and the correct port that it is listening on. If you are running VirtualBox, you should make sure your VM has two network interfaces. One should be a NAT interface that can be used to access the Internet, and the other should be a host-only interface to enable it to communicate with the host machine. For example, your NAT interface could be eth0 and have a 10.x IP address, and your host-only interface could be eth1 and have a 192.168.x IP address.

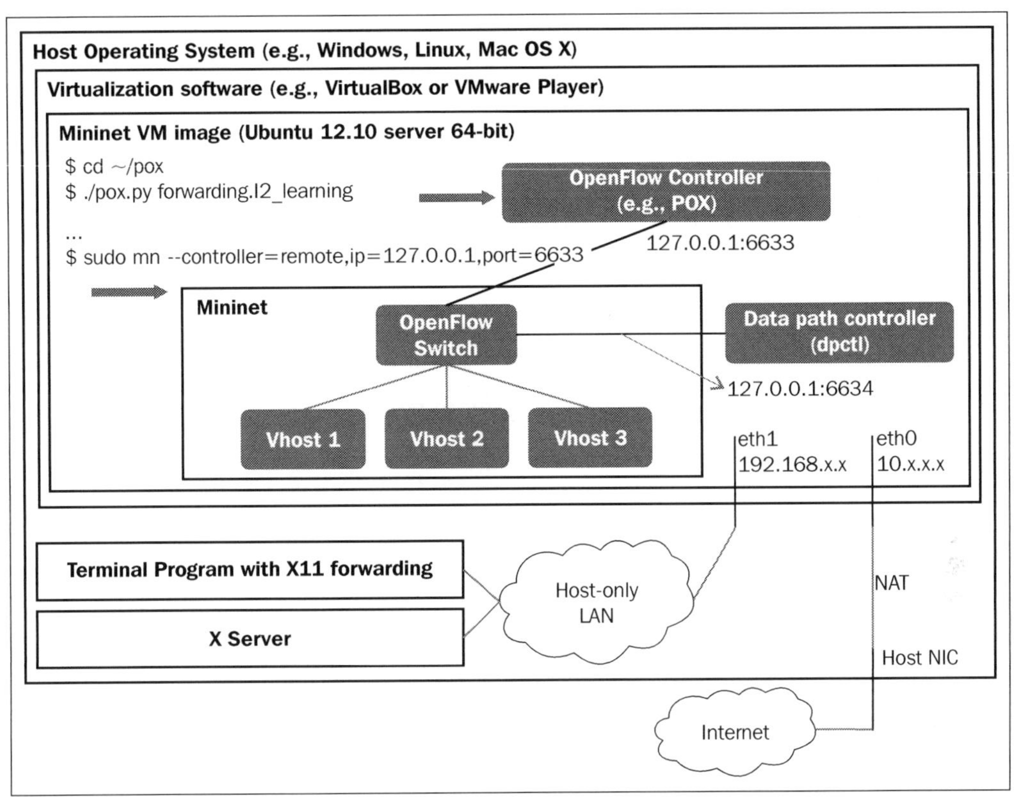

The OpenFlow laboratory environment and building blocks

In VirtualBox you should put the second network interface in the host-only mode. Select your VM image and go to the **settings** tab and then to **Network Adapter 2**. Select the **Enable adapter** box, and attach it to **host-only network**. This will allow you to easily access your VM through your host machine.

Now, you have to verify that you can connect from the host PC (your laptop) to the guest VM (OpenFlow laboratory) via SSH. From the virtual machine console, log in to the VM (username: `mininet`, password: `mininet`), then enter the following command:

```
$ ifconfig -a
```

You should see three interfaces (eth0, eth1, lo), both eth0 and eth1 should have IP addresses assigned. If this is not the case, type:

```
$ sudo dhclient ethX
```

Replace `ethX` with the name of the unnumbered interface. Note down the IP address of eth1 (probably the 192.168.x.x one) for the host-only network; you will need it later. Next, using your SSH client (PuTTY, terminal.app, and so on) log in to your Mininet VM. For example, on a Linux host, enter the following command:

```
$ ssh -X mininet@[eth1's IP address]
```

In order to use the X11 applications (xterm and Wireshark), the Xserver must be running. The next verification is the accessibility of the X server. Try starting up an X terminal using the `xterm` command:

```
$ xterm
```

and a new terminal window should appear. If you have succeeded, the environment of the OpenFlow laboratory will be ready and you can close the xterm. If you get a `xterm: Xt error: Can't open display` (or similar error), verify your X server installation.

Under Windows, the Xming server must be running, and you must make an SSH connection with X11 forwarding enabled. First, start Xming. Xming will not show any window, but you can verify that it is running by looking for its process in Window's task bar. Second, make an SSH connection with X11 forwarding enabled. If you are using PuTTY, you can connect to your OpenFlow laboratory by entering your VM's IP address (eth1) and enabling X11 forwarding. To enable X11 forwarding from PuTTY's GUI, go to **PuTTYConnection | SSH | X11**, then click on **Enable X11 Forwarding**, as shown in the following screenshot:

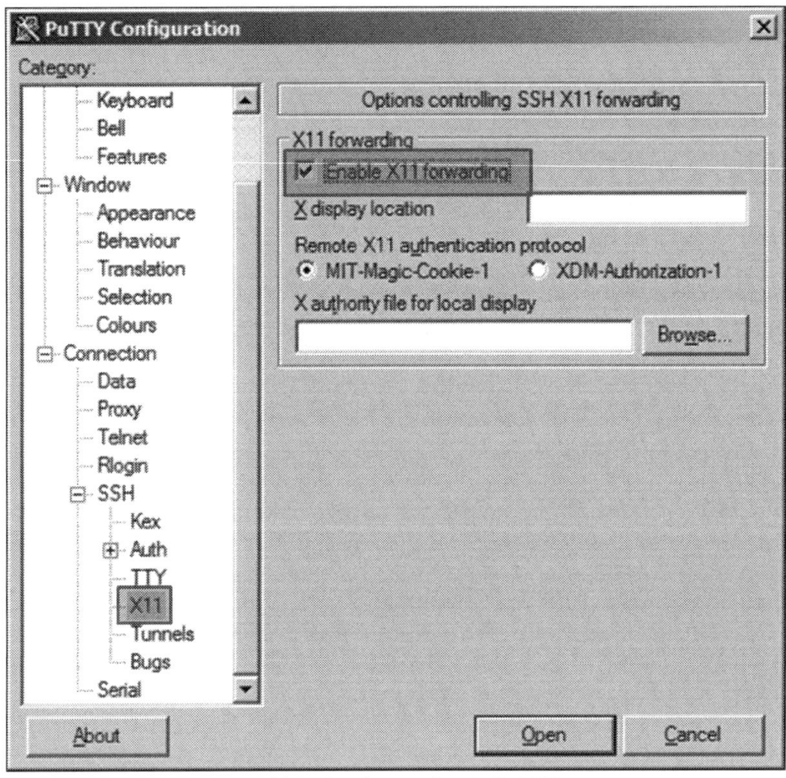

Enabling X11 forwarding in PuTTY

Alternatively, you can install X11 into the VM itself (that is, inside your OpenFlow laboratory VM). To install X11 and a simple window manager, log in to the VM console window (username: `mininet`, password: `mininet`) and type:

```
$ sudo apt-get update
$ sudo apt-get install xinit flwm
```

Now, you should be able to start an X11 session in the VM console window by typing:

```
$ startx
```

After establishing an SSH connection to your OpenFlow laboratory VM and logging in to it (username: `mininet`, password: `mininet`), you can start the sample Mininet network by entering the following command line:

```
$ sudo mn --topo single,3 --mac --switch ovsk --controller remote
```

Note that since you have not started any OpenFlow controller, you will get an error message like `unable to contact the remote controller at 127.0.0.1:6633`. Since the X11 forwarding is also enabled, you can start Wireshark to be able to capture the OpenFlow traffic. You can start Wireshark by entering the following command in your terminal (PuTTY):

```
mininet@mininet-vm:~$ wireshark &
```

This will open the Wireshark GUI and you can start capturing the network traffic and filtering the OpenFlow traffic as explained in *Chapter 2, Implementing the OpenFlow Switch*.

Now you can start your remote OpenFlow controller. This controller is in fact running inside your OpenFlow laboratory VM. So you need to go to your VM console and enter the following commands:

```
mininet@mininet-vm:~$ cd pox
mininet@mininet-vm:~/pox$ ./pox.py forwarding.l2_learning
```

and after a while your OpenFlow soft-switch in the Mininet will get connected to this controller. The output of your POX controller should look like the following:

```
POX 0.0.0 / Copyright 2011 James McCauley
DEBUG:core:POX 0.0.0 going up...
DEBUG:core:Running on CPython (2.7.3/Sep 26 2012 21:51:14)
INFO:core:POX 0.0.0 is up.
This program comes with ABSOLUTELY NO WARRANTY.  This program is
free software, and you are welcome to redistribute it under certain
conditions.
Type 'help(pox.license)' for details.
DEBUG:openflow.of_01:Listening for connections on 0.0.0.0:6633
INFO:openflow.of_01:[Con 1/1] Connected to 00-00-00-00-00-01
DEBUG:forwarding.l2_learning:Connection [Con 1/1]
Ready.
POX>
```

The debug messages of POX show that your OpenFlow switch is connected to the POX (OpenFlow controller) and behaves as an L2 learning switch. This will conclude the setup of our OpenFlow laboratory. We managed to set up a network using Mininet and also starting a remote OpenFlow controller (POX) as an environment for Net App development. In *Chapter 5, Net App Development*, we use this laboratory setup for our sample Net App development. In the next section, we will introduce another setup based on the OpenDaylight project.

OpenDaylight

OpenDaylight is a Linux foundation collaborative project (`www.opendaylight.org`), in which a community has come together to fill the need for an open and reference framework for programmability and control through an open source SDN solution. It combines open community developers, open source code, and project governance that guarantees an open, community decision-making process on business and technical issues. OpenDaylight can be a core component within any SDN architecture. Building upon an open source SDN controller enables users to reduce operational complexity, extend the lifetime of their existing network infrastructure, and enable new services and capabilities only available with SDN. The mission statement of OpenDaylight project can be read as, "OpenDaylight facilitates a community-led industry-supported open source framework, including code and architecture, to accelerate and advance a common, robust Software-Defined Networking platform". OpenDaylight is open to anyone. Anyone can develop and contribute code, get elected to the Technical Steering Committee (TSC), get voted onto the Board, or help steer the project forward in any number of ways. OpenDaylight will be composed of numerous projects. Each project will have contributors, committers, and one committer elected by their peers to be the Project Lead. The initial TSC and project leads will be composed of the experts who developed the code that has been originally contributed to the project. This ensures the community gets access to the experts most familiar with the contributed code to ramp up and provide mentorship to new community participants. Among initial bootstrap projects, OpenDaylight (ODL) controller is one of the early projects, which we will introduce in the next section and then we set up our environment for ODL-based Net App development.

ODL controller

The OpenDaylight (ODL) controller is a highly available, modular, extensible, scalable, and multi-protocol controller infrastructure built for SDN deployment on modern heterogeneous multi-vendor networks. The model driven **Service Abstraction Layer** (**SAL**) provides the needed abstractions to support multiple Southbound protocols (for example, OpenFlow) via plugins. The application oriented extensible north-bound architecture provides a rich set of Northbound APIs via RESTful web services for loosely coupled applications and OSGi services for co-located applications. The OSGi framework, upon which the controller platform is built, is responsible for the modular and extensible nature of the controller and also provides the versioning and life-cycle management for OSGi modules and services. The OpenDaylight controller supports not only the OpenFlow protocol, but also other open protocols to allow communication with devices which have OpenFlow and/or respective agents. It also includes a Northbound API to allow customer applications (software), which will work with the controller in controlling the network.

ODL is developed using Java and as a JVM it can run on any hardware platform and OS provided it supports Java JVM 1.7 and higher. The architecture of ODL is shown in the following figure:

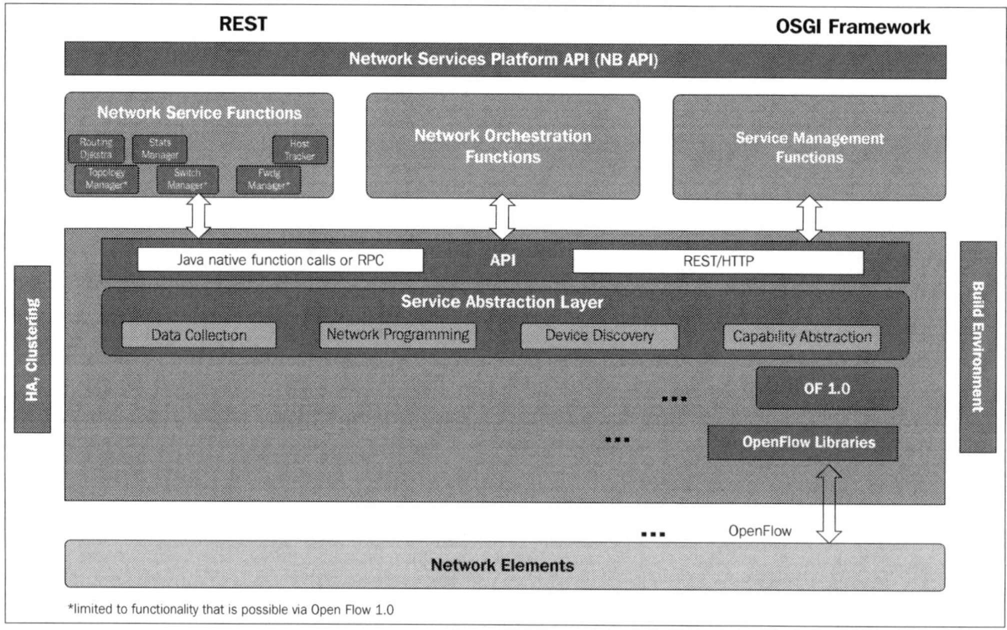

Architecture of ODL Controller

The Southbound ODL controller can support multiple protocols as plugins (for example, OpenFlow 1.0, PCE, BGP-LS, and so on). It currently supports OpenFlow 1.0. Other OpenDaylight contributors would add to those as part of their contributions/projects. These modules are dynamically linked into a **Service Abstraction Layer** (**SAL**). The SAL exposes services to which the modules in the higher layer serve. The SAL figures out how to fulfill the requested service irrespective of the underlying protocol used between the controller and the network elements (OpenFlow switch). This provides investment protection to the applications as the OpenFlow and other protocols evolve over time. The information regarding capabilities and reachability of the network devices is stored and managed by the Topology Manager. The other components (for example, ARP handler, Host Tracker, Device Manager, and Switch Manager) help in generating the topology database for the Topology Manager. The Switch Manager API holds the details of the network element. As a network element is discovered, its attributes (for example, what switch/router it is, SW version, capabilities, and so on) are stored in the database by the Switch Manager. The controller exposes open Northbound APIs, which are used by the applications. ODL controller supports the OSGi framework and bidirectional REST for the Northbound API. OSGi framework is used for applications that will run in the same address space as the controller while the REST (web-based) API is used for apps that do not run in the same address space (or even the same hardware/software platform) as the controller. The business logic and algorithms reside in the Net Apps. These Net Apps use the controller to gather network intelligence, runs its algorithm to do analytics, and then use the controller to orchestrate the new rules throughout the network. The ODL controller supports a cluster-based high availability model. There are several instances of the ODL controller, which logically act as one logical controller. This not only gives a fine grain redundancy, but also allows a scale-out model for linear scalability. The ODL controller has a built-in GUI. The GUI is implemented as an application using the same Northbound API as would be available for any other user application.

For more information about the architecture, development infrastructure, library description, and API references, please refer to ODL controller wiki page, which is located at: `http://wiki.opendaylight.org/view/OpenDaylight_Controller:Programmer_Guide`.

ODL-based SDN laboratory

In this section, we set up our SDN laboratory (with built-in OpenFlow support) using ODL controller. Our procedure assumes that you are installing ODL controller on your local Linux machine and you will use the Mininet VM (as detailed in the previous sections) to create a virtual network. Our host operating system is Windows 7 Enterprise and therefore throughout this section we will use VMware Player to host another virtual machine (Ubuntu 12.04) for ODL controller. The settings of our VM are as follows:

- 2 CPUs, 2 GB RAM, and 20 GB disk space.
- Bridged NIC, that puts the VM on the same network as your NIC. You can bind to wireless or wired. So if your physical host like your laptop is on 192.168.0.10/24, a VM in bridged mode would get 192.168.0.11/24 or whatever your DHCP server assigns to it. The point is to have the VM remain on the same sub network as your host computer.

After logging in to your VM, you have to download the following pre-requisite software:

- JVM 1.7 or higher, for example, OpenJDK 1.7 (`JAVA_HOME` should be set to the environment variable)
- Git to pull the ODL controller from the Git repository
- Maven

Install the dependencies and pull down the code using Git:

```
$ sudo apt-get update
$ sudo apt-get install maven git openjdk-7-jre openjdk-7-jdk
$ git clone http://git.opendaylight.org/gerrit/p/controller.git
$ cd controller/opendaylight/distribution/opendaylight/
$ mvn clean install
$ cd target/distribution.opendaylight-0.1.0-SNAPSHOT-osgipackage/
opendaylight
```

This will install the required tools and get the ODL controller from the Git repository. Then Maven will build and install the ODL controller. Apache Maven is a build automation tool used primarily for Java projects. Please note that building ODL controller takes a few minutes to be completed.

If your Maven build fails with a `Out Of Memory error: PermGen Space` error, re-run Maven using the `-X` switch to enable full debug logging. This is due to a memory leak somewhere in the Maven build and is being tracked as a bug. Instead of `mvn clean install` you can run `maven clean install -DskipTests` and it will skip the integration tests that seem to be the source of the garbage collector's leak. You can also address this error by setting maven options:

```
$ export MAVEN_OPTS="-Xmx512m -XX:MaxPermSize=256m"
```

The summary at the end of Maven build, will report the successful build of ODL controller along with the elapsed time and allocated/available memory. Before running the ODL controller, you have to set up the `JAVA_HOME` environment variable. The current value of `JAVA_HOME` can be viewed with `echo $JAVA_HOME` command. It will likely be undefined. Export the `JAVA_HOME` environment variable. You can write it to `.bashrc`, (located in the user home directory) to have it be persistent through reboots and logins. Place `JAVA_HOME=/usr/lib/jvm/java-1.7.0-openjdk-amd64` at the bottom of your `~/.bashrc` file or for a one time set:

```
$ export JAVA_HOME=/usr/lib/jvm/java-1.7.0-openjdk-i386 (or -amda64)
```

You can start the ODL controller by changing the current directory to the location where the ODL binary is available and start it by `run.sh`:

```
$ cd ~/controller/opendaylight/distribution/opendaylight/target/
distribution.opendaylight-0.1.0-SNAPSHOT-osgipackage/opendaylight
$ ./run.sh
```

ODL controller needs a couple of minutes to get all of its modules loaded. You can point your browser to 127.0.0.1:8080 to open the ODL controller web interface (see the following screenshot). The default user name and password is `admin` (username: `admin`, password: `admin`):

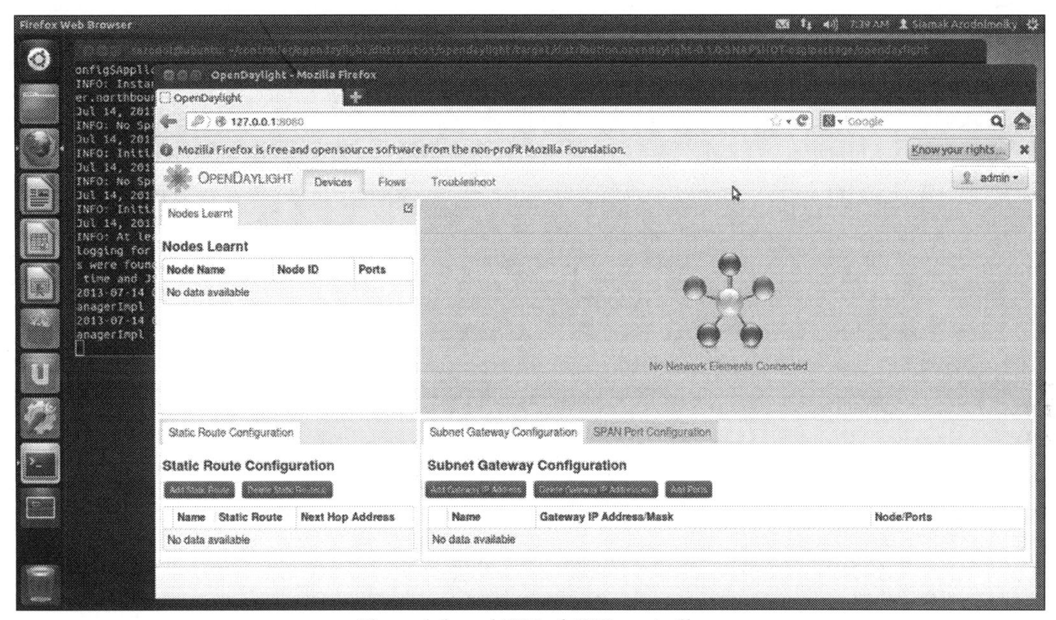

The web-based GUI of ODL controller

Now that we have the ODL controller up and running, we can point the OpenFlow switch of our OpenFlow laboratory to this controller. ODL controller has been tested against the Mininet VM, which is part of our OpenFlow laboratory. Launch the Mininet VM with VMPlayer, VirtualBox, or another virtualization application. Log in to the Mininet VM (username: `mininet`, password: `mininet`). Determine the IP address of the server hosting ODL controller (for example, `$ ifconfig -a`), and use it to start a virtual network:

```
mininet@mininet-vm:~$ sudo mn --controller=remote,ip=controller-ip --topo
single,3
```

Mininet will connect to the OpenDaylight controller and set up a switch and three hosts connected to it, as shown in the following screenshot:

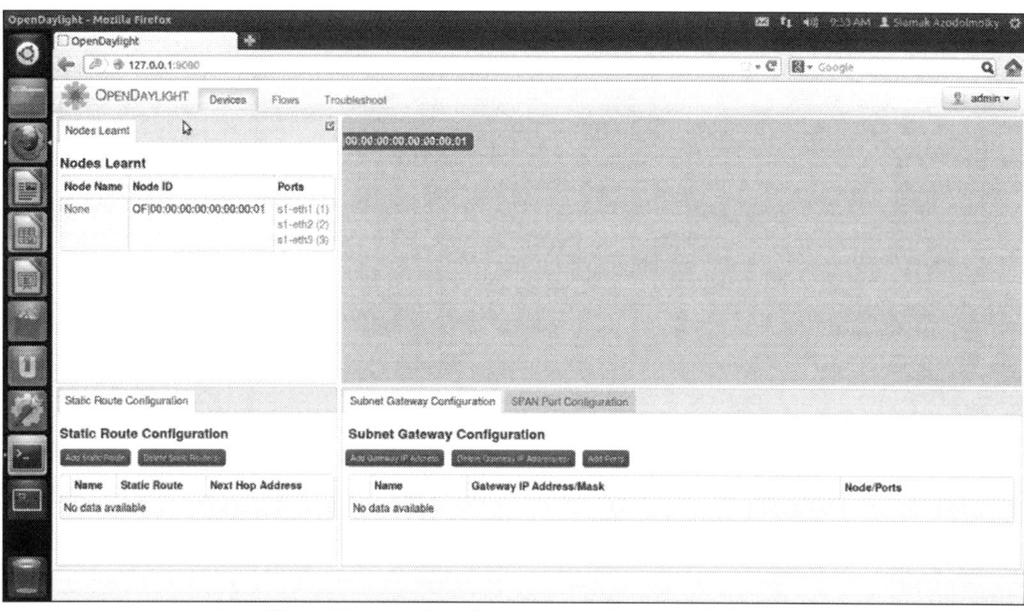

The GUI of ODL controller after setting up the network in Mininet

When you point an OpenFlow switch at the OpenDaylight controller, it will pop up as a device waiting to be configured. The data path ID is the unique key identifier made up of the switch MAC and an ID assigned by the controller. Mininet will use all zeroes with a one at the end. OpenFlow uses LLDP for topology discovery by using packet_out, an instruction in which the controller tells the forwarding element to do something like send an LLDP discovery. Next, specify the action for the **flowmod** (**Flow Modification**). The following screenshot shows part of a web-based form that collects the parameter for a flow entry, which can be installed in the flow table of OpenFlow switches. Here we choose the output port. Remember, OpenFlow only forwards what you instruct it to do, so either add rules to handle 0×0806 Ethernet type traffic for ARP broadcast requests and unicast replies or delete the Ethernet type default IPv4 0×0800 value when you add a flowmod. You also need to set up a match on traffic from port 1 with an action to forward to port 2 along with the return traffic of matching port 2 with an output action of port 1. You can specify reserved ports like normal, controller, flood, and all of the others listed in the drop-down boxes from the OpenFlow v1.0 specification. Choose an action that can be logical or physical. Logical tend to be named with symbolic representation while physical is numeric. Ports are learned by the switch sending configuration information and also updated if a port or link goes down. By adding the proper flows in the flow table of S1, you can establish a path between hosts and check it by pinging those hosts in Mininet. For troubleshooting you can use dpctl or Wireshark, which was covered earlier in this chapter and also *Chapter 2, Implementing the OpenFlow Switch*.

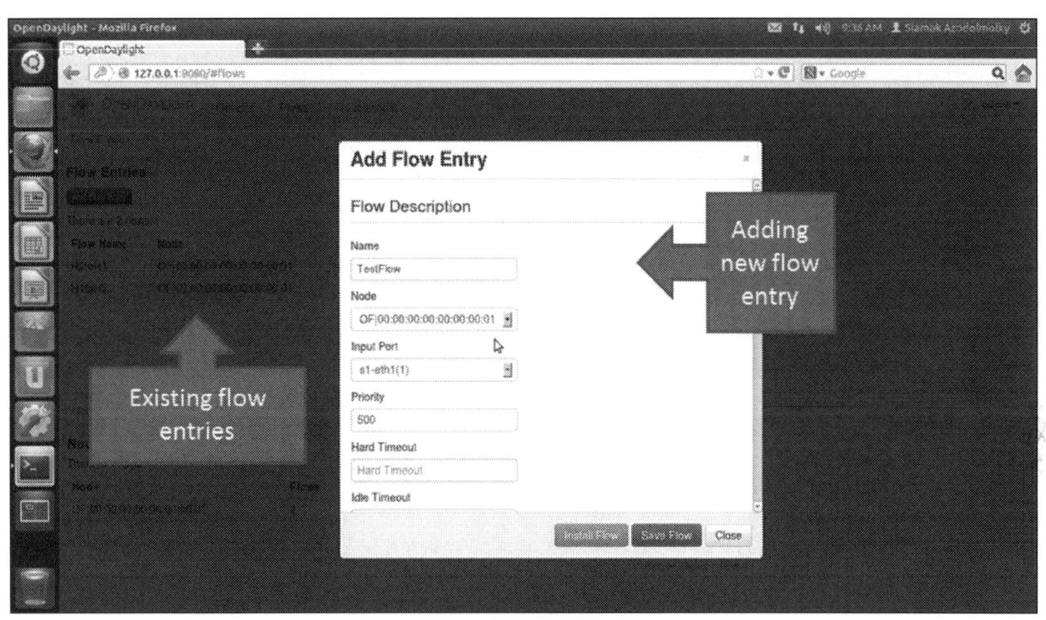

Adding new flow entry dialog box

Summary

In this chapter we provided a detailed description on our OpenFlow laboratory based on the Mininet and its role as a network emulator that can be interfaced to the remote controllers (POX). This setup is the development infrastructure, upon which we can utilize the Northbound API of the OpenFlow controllers (for example, POX) to develop Net Apps in the next chapter. Furthermore, we presented the OpenDaylight project and its boot strap controller (that is, ODL controller), which can be used as an SDN controller for our development environment. ODL controller and its northbound interface, which was also interfaced to the Mininet network emulator, is another promising environment, which we will use in the next chapter for sample Net App development.

5
"Net App" Development

Up to this point, we have covered the details about OpenFlow functionalities, and the role of OpenFlow switch and OpenFlow controllers in the SDN ecosystem. In *Chapter 4, Setting Up the Environment*, we setup our development environment and in this chapter we go through some network applications (Net Apps) using the POX OpenFlow controller and also the OpenDaylight controller that we introduced and setup in the previous chapter. Please note that the potentials and capabilities of OpenFlow controllers are more than the sample Net Apps that we will introduce in this chapter. However, the goal here is to give an initial push towards the basic steps in developing Net Apps using OpenFlow framework. In the first part of this chapter, we will start with our OpenFlow laboratory (based on Mininet) and go through the operation of an Ethernet hub, an Ethernet learning switch, and a simple firewall. Then, we will go through the details of a learning switch over the OpenDaylight controller.

Net App 1 – an Ethernet learning switch

Using our Mininet-based OpenFlow laboratory, we are going to set up a simple network consisting of an OpenFlow switch, three hosts, and an OpenFlow controller (POX). The topology of the network is shown in the following figure:

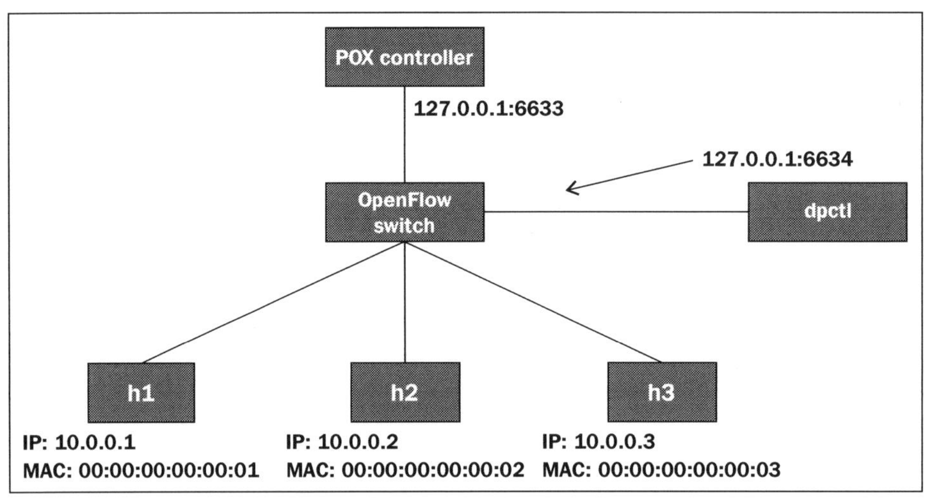

Experimental network topology in our OpenFlow laboratory using Mininet.

In addition to the POX controller, we also use the `dpctl` utility program to examine the flow table of the OpenFlow switch. As mentioned earlier, OpenFlow switches usually are listening on port 6634, which is considered for the `dpctl` (data path controller) channel. Even without an OpenFlow controller, we can use the `dpctl` utility program to communicate with the OpenFlow switch in our OpenFlow laboratory and inspect flow table entries, or modify flows. In order to set up the network topology, which is depicted in previous figure inside our Mininet OpenFlow laboratory, we start Mininet with the following command line parameters:

```
mininet@mininet-vm:~$ sudo mn --topo single,3 --mac --switch ovsk --
controller remote
```

Note that Mininet reports that it is not able to connect to the remote controller at 127.0.0.1:6633 (that is localhost:6633).

```
*** Adding controller
Unable to connect the remote controller at 127.0.0.1:6633
```

In fact, since we have not started any POX controller so far, the OpenFlow switch is not able to connect to the remote controller (as indicated by `--controller remote` in the command line parameters of the Mininet launcher). Please note that `--controller remote` by default refers to an OpenFlow controller located on localhost (that is 127.0.0.1). You can check the IP address and MAC address of h1 (and other hosts) using the following command:

```
mininet> h1 ifconfig
```

Now we can try to check the connectivity among the hosts (that is h1, h2, and h3) using the `pingall` command of Mininet:

```
mininet> pingall
```

The following will be the output:

```
*** Ping: testing ping reachability
h1 -> X X
h2 -> X X
h3 -> X X
*** Results: 100% dropped (6/6 lost)
```

These results show that the hosts (in spite of being physically connected to each other) in the current topology are not logically connected (are not reachable) to each other through the switch due to lack of any flow entry rule in the flow table of the switch. We can dump the content of the flow table of the OpenFlow switch using the following command (you need to establish an SSH terminal connection to your Mininet VM to issue this command):

```
mininet@mininet-vm:~$ dpctl dump-flows tcp:127.0.0.1:6634
```

The following will be the output:

```
status reply (xid=0xf36abb08): flags=none type=1 (flow)
```

Before attaching the POX controller to our network topology, in which the controller will play the role of an Ethernet hub, we quickly review the operation of an Ethernet hub. An Ethernet hub (that is an active hub, multiport repeater) is a device for connecting multiple Ethernet devices together and making them act as a single network segment. It has multiple input/output ports, in which a signal introduced at the input of any port appears at the output of every port except the original incoming one. No forwarding information is stored in the switch. The hub functionality is implemented in the `hub.py` code of POX distribution (developed by *James McCauley*). This program (along with the L2 learning switch) is located at the `~/pox/pox/forwarding` directory.

Looking at hub.py, we can find the launch method, which simply adds a listener for OpenFlow switches to connect to it:

```
def launch ():
    core.openflow.addlisternetByName("connectionUp", _handle_
ConnectionUp)
    log.info("Hub running.")
```

The _handle_connectionUp method, which is another method in hub.py, simply generates an OpenFlow message for the OpenFlow switch. The action, which is appended to the message, simply floods the packet on all ports of the OpenFlow switch (except the incoming port). The generated message is then sent to the OpenFlow switch in our experimental network topology:

```
def _handle_ConnectionUp (event):
    msg= of.ofp_flow_mod()
    msg.actions.append(of.ofp_action_output(port= of.OFPP_FLOOD))
    event.connection.send(msg)
    log.info("Hubifying %s", dpidToStr(event.dpid))
```

So the event handler (that is _handle_ConnectionUp), simply receives an event from the OpenFlow switch and then caches a *Flooding* rule inside the flow table of the switch. Let us start the POX controller with the following hub functionality:

```
mininet@mininet-vm:~/pox$ ./pox.py forwarding.hub
```

The following will be the output:

```
POX POX 0.0.0 / Copyright 2011 James McCauley
INFO:forwarding.hub:Hub running.
DEBUG:core:POX 0.0.0 going up...
DEBUG:core:Running on CPython (2.7.3/Sep 26 2012 21:51:14)
INFO:core:POX 0.0.0 is up.
This program comes with ABSOLUTELY NO WARRANTY.  This program is
free software, and you are welcome to redistribute it under certain
conditions.
Type 'help(pox.license)' for details.
DEBUG:openflow.of_01:Listening for connections on 0.0.0.0:6633
Ready.
POX> INFO:openflow.of_01:[Con 1/1] Connected to 00-00-00-00-00-01
INFO:forwarding.hub:Hubifying 00-00-00-00-00-01
```

Note that upon the start of the POX controller (functioning as an Ethernet hub), an information message confirms that the OpenFlow switch is connected to the POX controller. The data path identification (`dpid`) of the switch is also printed out as `00-00-00-00-00-01`. You can return back to the Mininet command prompt and issue the *net* command to see the network elements, in which `c0` (controller 0) will also be printed out. Now, we can try to *pingall* hosts in our topology using the `pingall` command of Mininet.

```
mininet> pingall
```

The following will be the output:

```
*** Ping: testing ping reachability
h1 -> h2 h3
h2 -> h1 h3
h3 -> h1 h2
*** Results: 0% dropped (0/6 lost)
```

And we can also use `dpctl` (from our new SSH terminal) to see the content of the flow table of our OpenFlow switch:

```
mininet@mininet-vm:~$ dpctl dump-flows tcp:127.0.0.1:6634
```

The following will be the output:

```
stats_reply (xid=0x2f0cd1c7): flags=none type=1(flow)
  cookie=0, duration_sec=800s, duration_nsec=467000000s, table_id=0,
priority=32768, n_packets=24, n_bytes=1680,
idle_timeout=0,hard_timeout=0,actions=FLOOD
```

So, we started our experimental network topology in Mininet and made its OpenFlow switch get connected to the POX controller, which was behaving like an Ethernet hub. The interesting point about our first Net App is that just by 12 lines of code in Python (that is `hub.py`), we managed to perform the Ethernet hub functionality in the network.

Building the learning switch

Now, we change and enhance the behavior of our OpenFlow switch to an intelligent (learning) Ethernet switch. Let us review the operation of a learning switch. When a packet arrives to any port of the learning switch, it can learn that the sending host is located on the port on which the packet has arrived. So, it can simply maintain a lookup table that associates the MAC address of the host with the port on which they are connected to the switch. So the switch stores the source MAC address of the packet, along with the incoming port in its lookup table. Upon receiving a packet, the switch looks up the destination MAC address of the packet and in case of a match, the switch figures out the output port and instead of flooding the packet, it simply sends the packet to its correct destination host (through the looked up port). In the OpenFlow paradigm, each incoming packet basically generates a new rule in the flow table of the OpenFlow switch. In order to observe this behavior, we re-start our experimental network with the l2_learning switch (that is `l2_learning.py`) functionality. The learning switch algorithm, which is implemented in the `l2_learning.py` script, consists of the following steps:

- The first step is to use the source MAC address of the packet and the switch port to update the switching lookup table (that is the address/port table), maintained inside the controller as a hash table.
- The second step is to drop a certain type of the packets (packets with Ethertype of LLDP or packets with a bridge filtered destination address).
- In the third step, the controller checks if the destination address is a multicast address. In that case, the packet is simply flooded.
- If the destination MAC address of the packet is not already inside the address/port table (that is the hash table, which is maintained inside the controller), then the controller instructs the OpenFlow switch to flood the packet on all ports (except the incoming one).
- If the output port is the same as the input port, the controller instructs the switch to drop the packet to avoid loops.
- Otherwise the controller sends a flow table entry modification command (that is flow mod) to the switch, using the source MAC address and corresponding port, which instructs the switch that the future packets, which are addressed to that specific MAC address, will be sent to the associated output port (rather than flooding).

In order to see the learning switch behavior of our setup we first clean up the existing setup and start our experimental network again:

```
mininet@mininet-vm:~$ sudo mn -c
... (screen messages are removed)
```

```
mininet@mininet-vm:~$ sudo mn --topo single,3 --mac --switch ovsk --
controller remote
```

Now, using another SSH terminal, we connect to our Mininet VM and start the POX controller, which executes the Ethernet L2 (Layer 2) learning switch algorithm:

```
mininet@mininet-vm:~/pox$ ./pox.py forwarding.l2_learning
```

Upon startup of the POX controller, as the Ethernet hub case, we can observe that the OpenFlow switch will get connected to the controller. Now if we go back to the Mininet console and issue the `pingall` command, we will see that all hosts are reachable.

```
mininet> pingall
```

The following will be the output:

```
*** Ping: testing ping reachability
h1 -> h2 h3
h2 -> h1 h3
h3 -> h1 h2
*** Results: 0% dropped (0/6 lost)
```

So far, the behavior is like the Ethernet hub case. However, if we dump the flow table of the switch (using the `dpctl` program), we can observe a bunch of different flow table entries. In fact, the flow table entries show different destination MAC addresses along with the associated output ports that incoming packets addressed to that MAC should be forwarded to. For instance, packets addressed to `00:00:00:00:00:03` will be forwarded to the output port number 3.

```
mininet@mininet-vm:~$ dpctl dump-flows tcp:127.0.0.1:6634
```

The following will be the output:

```
stats_reply (xid=0xababe6ce): flags=none type=1(flow)
  cookie=0, duration_sec=7s, duration_nsec=912000000s, table_id=0,
priority=32768, n_packets=1, n_bytes=98,
idle_timeout=10,hard_timeout=30,icmp,dl_vlan=0xffff,dl_vlan_pcp=0x00,
dl_src=00:00:00:00:00:02,dl_dst=00:00:00:00:00:03,nw_src=10.0.0.2,nw_
dst=10.0.0.3,nw_tos=0x00,icmp_type=0,icmp_code=0,actions=output:3
...
...
 (more entries are not shown)
```

Let's take a look at the Python code (that is `l2_learning.py`), which implements the Ethernet learning switch functionality. The launch method as usual registers the `l2_learning` object with the core POX controller. Upon being instantiated, the `l2_learning` object adds a listener to ensure that it can handle connection up events from OpenFlow switches that connect to this controller. This object then instantiates the learning switch object and passes the connection event to that object (see the highlighted code in the following):

```
...
...
class l2_learning (EventMixin):
  """
  Waits for OpenFlow switches to connect and makes them learning
switches.
  """
  def __init__ (self, transparent):
    self.listenTo(core.openflow)
    self.transparent = transparent

  def _handle_ConnectionUp (self, event):
    log.debug("Connection %s" % (event.connection,))
    LearningSwitch(event.connection, self.transparent)


def launch (transparent=False):
  """
  Starts an L2 learning switch.
  """
  core.registerNew(l2_learning, str_to_bool(transparent))
```

Going through the *learning switch* object, we can observe that upon instantiation of the address/port, the hash table is created (that is `self.macToPort= {}`) a listener is registered for the packet-in messages (that is `connection.addListeners(self)`) and then we can see the packet-in handler method (that is `_handle_PacketIn (self, event)`). The learning switch algorithm portion of the code is as follows:

```
    self.macToPort[packet.src] = event.port
    if not self.transparent:
      if packet.type == packet.LLDP_TYPE or
      packet.dst.isBridgeFiltered():
        drop()
        return
      if packet.dst.isMulticast():
        flood()
      else:
```

```
        if packet.dst not in self.macToPort:
          log.debug("Port for %s unknown -- flooding" %
          (packet.dst,))
            flood()
        else:
        port = self.macToPort[packet.dst]
      if port == event.port:
        log.warning("Same port for packet from %s -> %s on %s.
        Drop." %
      (packet.src, packet.dst, port), dpidToStr(event.dpid))
      drop(10)
      return
      log.debug("installing flow for %s.%i -> %s.%i" %
      (packet.src, event.port, packet.dst, port))
      msg = of.ofp_flow_mod()
      msg.match = of.ofp_match.from_packet(packet)
      msg.idle_timeout = 10
      msg.hard_timeout = 30
      msg.actions.append(of.ofp_action_output(port = port))
      msg.buffer_id = event.ofp.buffer_id
    self.connection.send(msg)
```

The first step is to update the address/port hash table (that is `self.macToPort[packet.src] = event.port`). This will associate the MAC address of the sender to the switch port on which the packet has been received by the switch. Certain types of the packets are dropped. Multicast traffic is properly flooded. If the destination of the packet is not available in the address/port hash table, the packet is also flooded. If the input and output ports are the same, then the packet will be dropped to avoid loop (`if port == event.port:`). Finally, a proper flow table entry gets installed inside the flow table of the OpenFlow switch. In summary, the `l2_learning.py` program implements the required logic and algorithm to change the behavior of our OpenFlow switch to an Ethernet learning switch one. In the next section, we will take one more step to change the learning switch to a simple firewall.

Net App 2 – A simple firewall

In this section, we take the learning switch Net App and extend it to make packet forwarding decisions based on simple firewall rules that we install at the OpenFlow controller (POX). We are following two important goals in this Net App development. The first one is to demonstrate how easy it is to change the behavior of the network device (OpenFlow switch) by just simply changing the Net App at the OpenFlow controller. The second goal is to give more information about POX controller. In our simple firewall Net App, we want the switch to make drop or forwarding decisions based on the value of the source MAC address of the packets. The experimental network will be the one that is shown in the previous figure. However, we augment the `l2_learning.py` Net App (that is L2 learning switch) to perform the functionality of a simple firewall. Therefore, we copy the `l2_learning.py` program with a new name (for instance, `simple_firewall.py`) and add the firewall logic and rules on top of the L2 learning switch intelligence. This extension simply checks the source MAC address of the incoming packets and based on the outcome of comparison with the firewall rules, it will forward or drop the packet. If the controller decides that the packet should be forwarded, then it proceeds to perform the L2 switching functions as earlier. So, the new step after updating the address/port table of the L2 learning switch will be:

- Check the source MAC address of the incoming packet against the firewall rules

This requires only a few simple additions to the learning switch code. First, we need a hash table to store the (switch, source MAC) pairs. It maps the (switch, source MAC) to a true or false logical value indicating whether the packet should be forwarded or dropped. The controller will decide to drop the incoming packet if there is a firewall entry that maps to false (that is `FirewallTable(switch, Source MAC) == False`), or if there is no firewall entry for that source MAC address in the firewall hash table. The controller will decide to forward the traffic only if there is a `FirewallTable` entry that maps to true. These checks can be added to the learning switch code as follows:

```
...
    # Initializing our FirewallTable
    self.firewallTable = {}
    # Adding some sample firewall rules
    self.AddRule('00-00-00-00-00-01',EthAddr('00:00:00:00:00:01'))
    self.AddRule('00-00-00-00-00-01',EthAddr('00:00:00:00:00:03'))
...
...
    # Check the Firewall Rules
    if self.CheckFirewallRule(dpidstr, packet.src) == False:
      drop()
      return
```

The `CheckFirewallRule` method simply performs the required firewalling operation. Basically it only returns `True` if the firewall table has a rule for the given source MAC address.

```
    # check if the incoming packet is compliant to the firewall rules
  before normal proceeding
    def CheckFirewallRule (self, dpidstr, src=0):
      try:
        entry = self.firewallTable[(dpidstr, src)]
        if (entry == True):
          log.debug("Rule (%s) found in %s: FORWARD",
          src, dpidstr)
        else:
          log.debug("Rule (%s) found in %s: DROP",
          src, dpidstr)
        return entry
        except KeyError:
        log.debug("Rule (%s) NOT found in %s: DROP",
        src, dpidstr)
      return False
```

In this example, the firewall rules are set in a way that only packets from MAC addresses `00:00:00:00:00:01` and `00:00:00:00:00:03` will be processed and forwarded by the switch, and other traffic is simply dropped. Now we can start Mininet and the POX controller with our firewall Net App as follows:

```
mininet@mininet-vm:~$ sudo mn --topo single,3 --mac --switch ovsk --
controller remote
...
```

Run the following command on another SSH terminal:

```
mininet@mininet-vm:~/pox$ ./pox.py log.level --DEBUG
forwarding.simple_firewall.py
```

Note that we have passed additional command line parameters to the POX controller to be able to see detailed debugging messages of the POX controller while running our firewall Net App. Since there is no rule in the firewall table that allows h2 to forward its traffic, we should expect that the `pingall` command confirms this expected behavior:

```
mininet> pingall
```

The following will be the output:

```
*** Ping: testing ping reachability
h1 -> X h3
h2 -> X X
h3 -> h1 X
*** Results: 66% dropped (4/6 lost)
```

We can also see from the POX debugging messages that the controller decided to forward or drop different packets depending on the value of the source MAC address of the incoming packets. It is also interesting to note that when the controller decides to forward a packet, it also caches a rule in the flow table of the OpenFlow switch that allows that packet to be forwarded. As long as that entry remains in the flow table, all packets that match the flow entry table can continue to be forwarded at the switch. This *caching* (that is limited duration of flow entry existence in the flow table of the switch) introduces some performance impact on the switch operation. By caching, we are referring to the availability of a flow entry in the flow table of the switch, which allows the high-speed forwarding of packets without any controller involvement. Forwarding performance is degraded when the first packet of a flow (traffic stream of packets) needs to wait for the forwarding decision of the controller. This effect is usually referred to as first packet delay of a flow. Let's have it this way: host 1 pings host 3. From the ping output we can observe that the first packet is observing high latency since the flow table of the switch is empty and the OpenFlow switch should contact the controller. After caching the instruction in the flow table of the switch, packets are forwarded by the switch. After about 30 seconds, the flow table entry expires and again we observe relatively higher latency between the two end hosts (which are h1 and h3) since once again the traffic is redirected to the controller. Following is the command:

```
mininet> h1 ping h3
```

The following will be the output:

```
PING 10.0.0.3 (10.0.0.3) 56(84) bytes of data.
64 bytes from 10.0.0.3: icmp_req=1 ttl=64 time=38.6 ms
64 bytes from 10.0.0.3: icmp_req=2 ttl=64 time=0.264 ms
64 bytes from 10.0.0.3: icmp_req=3 ttl=64 time=0.056 ms
...
64 bytes from 10.0.0.3: icmp_req=32 ttl=64 time=26.8 ms
64 bytes from 10.0.0.3: icmp_req=33 ttl=64 time=0.263 ms
64 bytes from 10.0.0.3: icmp_req=34 ttl=64 time=0.053 ms
```

Net App 3 – simple forwarding in OpenDaylight

In *Chapter 4, Setting Up the Environment,* we also set up an SDN laboratory based on the OpenDaylight controller. In this section we will go through a sample forwarding application, which is available on OpenDaylight distribution. The OpenDaylight controller includes a Net App called Simple Forwarding that lets you use the basic services for making forwarding decisions and installing flows across all devices on the OpenFlow network. This application discovers the presence of a host via ARP message and installs destination-only /32 entries across all switches in the network, along with the corresponding output ports towards that host. Please refer to *Chapter 4, Setting Up the Environment,* for instruction on setting up the SDN laboratory. However, please note that the Mininet network should be setup using the following command:

```
sudo mn --controller=remote,ip=<OpenDaylight IP> --topo tree,3
```

With OpenDaylight Controller and Mininet running as described in the previous chapter, log into the OpenDaylight web interface. Drag and drop devices to organize the topology into its logical arrangement (that is the tree topology), then save the configuration. Click on the **Add Gateway IP Address** button and add the IP and subnet of 10.0.0.254/8 (see the following screenshot). This will properly initiate the requests to the OpenFlow controller and update the flow table of switches accordingly.

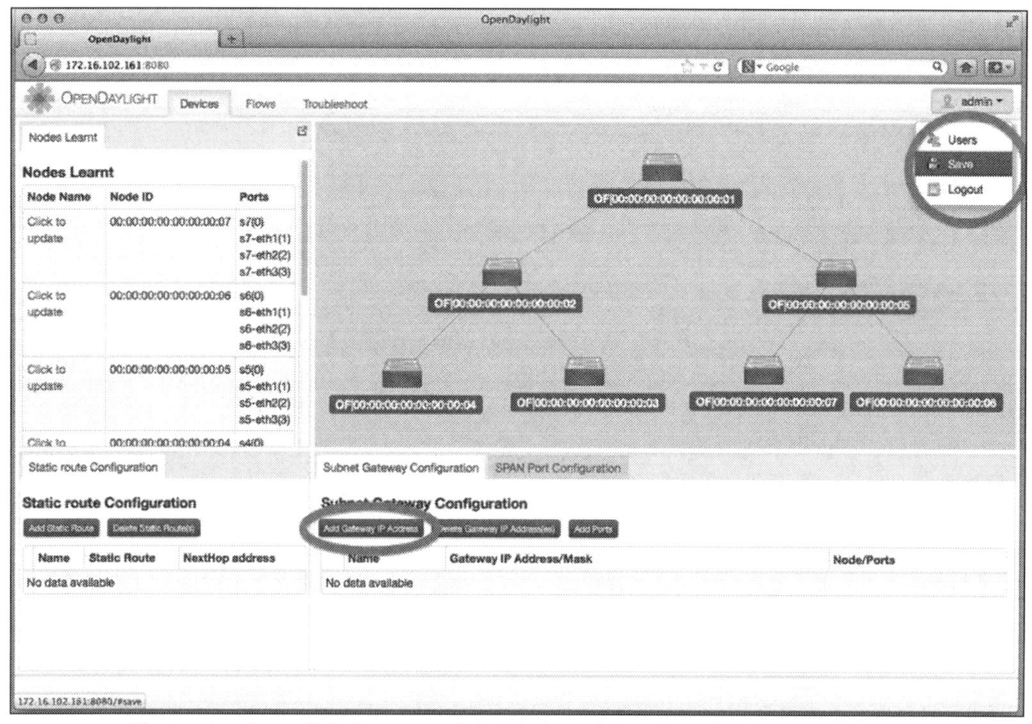

The tree topology of Mininet network inside the web interface of OpenDaylight GUI.

On the console where Mininet is running, issue the `pingall` command to confirm that all hosts are now reachable from one another. Click on the **Troubleshoot** tab and then load the flow details for one of the switches. View the port details (following screenshot).

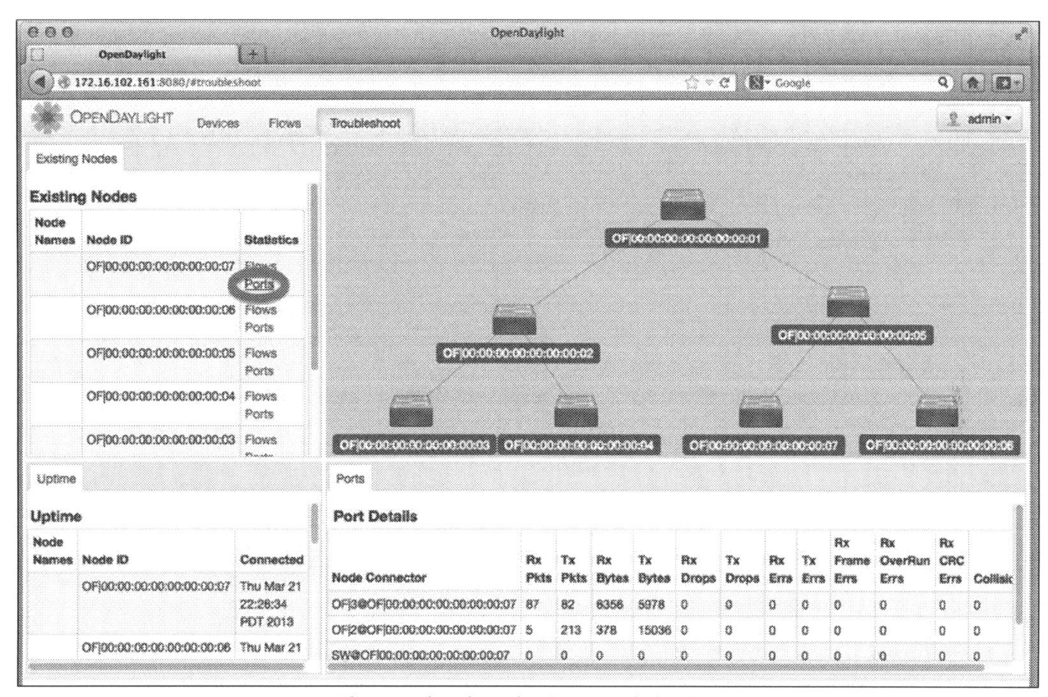

The port details in the OpenDaylight GUI.

On the OSGI console (the command line interface of the console, where the ODL controller had been started), type `ss simple`. You will see that the Simple Forwarding app is `ACTIVE`, as shown in the following figure:

Status of simple forwarding application in the OSGI console

Summary

In this chapter, we presented sample network applications, which utilized the OpenFlow and SDN controllers as a platform to perform networking applications. In particular, we started with a simple hub functionality over the POX controller and then we moved towards Layer 2 learning switching functionality. By adding more logic to this learning switch, we demonstrated how easily we can perform packet inspection as it could be done in a simple firewall by extending the learning switch. Finally, we showed simple packet forwarding Net App, which utilized the OpenDaylight SDN controller. In the next chapter, we will look at network virtualization and how to get a network slice.

6
Getting a Network Slice

In this chapter, network slicing with FlowVisor is discussed. The following topics will be covered:

- Network virtualization
- FlowVisor as an open source tool for OpenFlow based network slicing
- FlowVisor API, flow match, and slice action structures
- Network slicing using Mininet

Network virtualization

Network virtualization is a particular abstraction of the physical networking infrastructure that provides the support for multiple logical (virtual) network infrastructures (for example, a set of switches, routes, and links) on top of a common physical (real) infrastructure.

The analogy of network virtualization is depicted in the following figure:

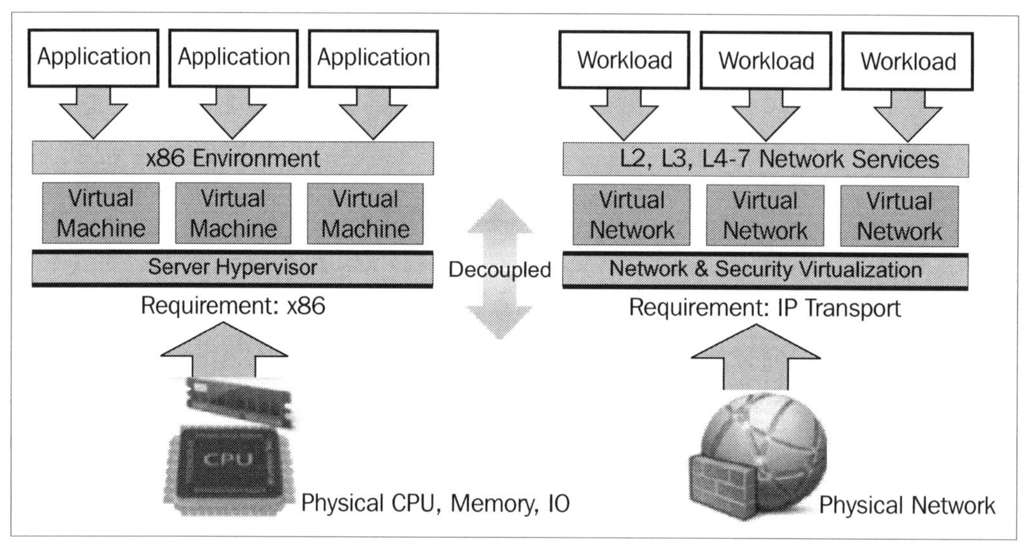

The analogy of computer virtualization and network virtualization

On the left side of this figure, we can see a conventional computer virtualization, which is the virtual machine environment. In this environment the physical processor (CPU), memory, and Input/output are abstracted by a hypervisor, on top of which, a virtual machine can be run. This hypervisor essentially ensures the isolation of access to underlying resources and resource management. Similarly, a physical network can also be virtualized. On the right side of the preceding figure, the network virtualization layer shown, is responsible for providing an isolated view of the physical network infrastructure. Building a virtual network requires the technology to build virtual nodes (for example, Xen Virtual Machine Monitor, Linux network namespaces, Kernel-based Virtual Machine (KVM), VMware, and VirtualBox). There are also other possible ways to create virtual links. These are essentially based on tunneling technology. One possibility is to get an Ethernet frame of a virtual node and encapsulate it in an IP packet that may travel through multiple hops in the network. This technique essentially provides a virtual Ethernet link using tunneling technology (for example, Ethernet Generic Routing Encapsulation (GRE) Tunneling, Virtual Extensible Local Area Network (VxLAN), Stateless Transport Tunneling (STT), among others). There are also technologies such as Open vSwitch that provide virtual switches. It's worth mentioning that **Software-defined Network (SDN)** separates the data plane and the control plane, but the goal of network virtualization is to construct multiple virtual networks on top of a physical networking infrastructure.

FlowVisor

An SDN can have some level of logical decentralization, with multiple logical controllers. An interesting type of proxy controller, called FlowVisor, can be utilized to add a level of network virtualization to OpenFlow networks and allow multiple controllers to simultaneously control overlapping sets of physical switches. Initially developed to allow experimental research to be conducted on deployed networks alongside production traffic, it also facilitates and demonstrates the ease of deploying new services in SDN environments. FlowVisor can be considered as a special purpose OpenFlow controller that acts as a transparent proxy between OpenFlow switches on one side and multiple OpenFlow controllers on the other side, as depicted in the following figure:

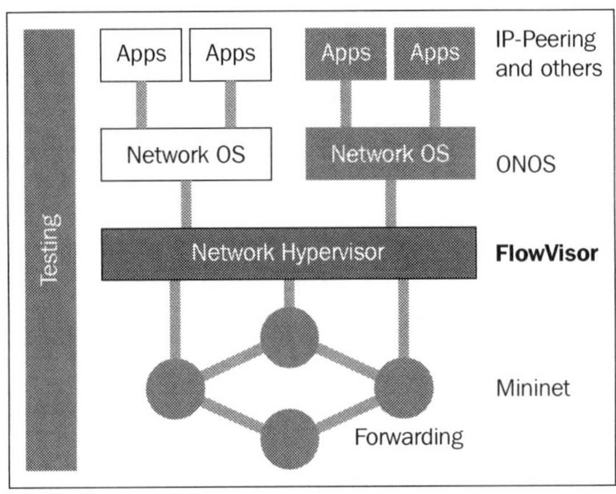

FlowVisor as a network slicer.

FlowVisor creates rich "slices" of network resources and delegates control of each slice to a different controller and also promotes isolation between slices. FlowVisor, originally developed at Stanford University, has been widely used in experimental Research and Education networks to support slicing where multiple experimenters get their own isolated slice of the infrastructure and control it using their own network OS and a set of control and management applications. FlowVisor enables you to conduct network research in real production environments and using real network traffic. As an open source proxy controller, you can customize the code to adapt to your needs; with a configuration and monitoring interface in JavaScript Object Notation (JSON) for users, and a Java programming language for developers, everyone has the ability to customize by opting to different services. You can freely and quickly experiment with SDN with all the foundational SDN functions that enable you to learn about network virtualization and test new methods for deploying services rapidly. Since it is based on open standards that can run on a multi-vendor infrastructure, it supports multiple vendors (for example, NEC, HP, Pronto, OVS, and so on), as well as multiple guest network OSes (for example, OpenFlow controllers).

> You can find more information about FlowVisor and source code at: `http://www.flowvisor.org`. The instruction for installation from binary is given here: `http://github.com/OPENNETWORKINGLAB/flowvisor/wiki/Installation-from-Binary`

FlowVisor API

FlowVisor is able to provide slices of network resources and convey the control of each slice to a different OpenFlow controller. Slices can be defined by any combination of packet contents from layer 1 to 4 including:

- Switch ports (layer 1)
- Source/destination Ethernet MAC address or Ethernet type (layer 2)
- Source/destination IP addresses or type (layer 3)
- Source/destination TCP/UDP port or ICMP code/type (layer 4)

FlowVisor provides and enforces slice isolation. This isolation means that the data traffic in one slice cannot be captured by hosts in the other slice. The FlowVisor API is transiting from XML-RPC to JSON. The XML-RPC API will remain as is but in a deprecated state and eventually it will be removed from the API. FlowVisor users are advised to migrate any of their dependencies on the FlowVisor API to the JSON interface. The API syntax may change in some areas. Please check the latest FlowVisor documentation for the updated syntax. A command line tool can be used to access the API of FlowVisor. This tool is named `fvctl`. For example, the following command line shows how the `list-slices` is invoked using the `fvctl` command line tool:

```
$ fvctl list-slices
```

The FlowVisor API includes the following commands:

- The `list-slices` command can be used to list the currently configured slices.
- The `list-slice-info <slicename>` command shows the URL address of the control, which controls the specified slicename. In addition, the information of the slice owner, who has created the slice and his/her contact information will be shown.
- The `add-slice <slicename> <controller_url> <email>` command creates a new slice. The slicename cannot contain any of the following special characters, !, :, =, [,], or new lines. The format of the URL address of the controller is specified as tcp:hostname[:port] like tcp:127.0.0.1:12345. The default port (if not specified) is 6633. The e-mail address is used as the administrative contact point of the slice.

- The `update-slice <slicename> <key> <value>` command enables a slice user to modify the information, which is associated with their slice. Only `contact_email`, `controller_host`, and `controller_port` can be changed as of writing this.
- The `list-flowspace` command prints the flow-based slice policy roles, which are also called flowspace.
- The `remove-slice <slicename>` command deletes a slice and releases all of the flowspace, which is corresponding to the slice.
- The `update-slice-password <slicename>` command changes the password, which is associated to the `slicename` parameter.
- The `add-flowspace <NAME> <DPID> <PRIORITY> <FLOW_MATCH> <SLICEACTIONS>` command creates a new slice policy rule (flowspace) with its given NAME. The format of DPID, FLOW_MATCH, and SLICEACTIONS are explained in the following subsections.
- The `update-flowspace <NAME> <DPID> <PRIORITY> <FLOW_MATCH> <SLICEACTIONS>` command modifies the slice policy rule, which is indicated by the NAME parameter with a new rule with the specified parameters. The format of DPID, FLOW_MATCH, and SLICEACTIONS are explained in the following subsections.
- The `remove-flowspace <NAME>` command deletes the policy rule with the specified NAME.

FLOW_MATCH structure

How a flow matches an incoming packet is explained in the following field assignments. The `FLOW_MATCH` field is treated as a wildcard if any of these assignment statements are removed from the syntax of a flow. Therefore, if all of these fields are removed, then the resulting flow matches all packets; `all` or `any` can be used to specify a flow that matches all packets.

- The `in_port=port_no` assignment matches the physical port `port_no` with the port number of the incoming packet. Switch ports are numbered, as they are listed by the `fvctl getDeviceInfo DPID` command.
- The `dl_vlan=vlan` assignment matches the IEEE 802.1Q virtual LAN tag `vlan` with the value of the VLAN in the incoming packet. In order to match packets, which are not tagged with a VLAN, you can specify `0xffff` as the value of the `vlan` parameter. Otherwise, specify a numeric value between 0 and 4095 (inclusive) as the 12-bit VLAN ID to match.

- The `dl_src=mac` assignment matches the Ethernet source MAC address `mac`. This MAC address should be specified as 6 pairs of hexadecimal digits delimited by colons, like `00:0A:E4:25:6B:B0`.
- The `dl_dst=mac` assignment matches the Ethernet destination MAC address `mac`.
- The `dl_type=ethertype` assignment matches Ethernet protocol type `ethertype`, which should be specified as an integer between 0 and 65535 (inclusive) either in decimal or as a hexadecimal number prefixed by 0x (for instance to match ARP packets, you can specify 0x0806 as the value of `ethertype`).
- The `nw_src=ip[/netmask]` assignment matches the IPv4 source address `ip` (specified as an IP address, for example 192.168.0.1). The optional `netmask` provides a mechanism to only match on the prefix of an IPv4 address. The `netmask` is specified as CIDR-style, that is, for example, something like 192.168.1.0/24.
- The `nw_dst=ip[/netmask]` assignment matches the IPv4 destination address `ip` with the destination address of the incoming packet. `netmask` allows the prefix matching (for instance 192.168.1.0/24).
- The `nw_proto=proto` assignment matches the IP protocol type `proto` field, which should be specified as an integer value between 0 and 255 (for instance 6 to match the TCP packets).
- The `nw_tos=tos/dscp` assignment matches the ToS/DSCP field of IPv4 header value `tos/dscp` with the same quantity of the incoming packets. This value should be specified as an integer value between 0 and 255.
- The `tp_src=port` assignment matches the transport-layer (for instance TCP, UDP, or ICMP) source port `port`. It should be specified as an integer value between 0 and 65535 (in the case of TCP or UDP) or between 0 and 255 (in the case of ICMP).
- The `tp_dst=port` assignment matches the transport-layer destination `port`. The value should be in the same range that was mentioned for the transport layer source port.

Slice actions structure

Slice actions is a list of slices that have control over a specific flowspace. This list is comma separated and the slice actions are of the form Slice:slicename1=perm[Slice:slicename2=perm[...]]. Each slice possibly has three types of access permissions over a flowspace, which are: DELEGATE, READ, and WRITE. Permissions are currently specified as an integer bitmask value. The assignment is: DELEGATE=1, READ=2, WRITE=4. So, `Slice:alice=5,bob=2` would give DELEGATE and WRITE (1+4 = 5) permissions to the alice's slice and only read permission to bob.

FlowVisor slicing

In this section, you will learn how to slice your OpenFlow network, construct logical networks over a physical infrastructure, and have each slice controlled by an OpenFlow controller. You will also learn, during this process, the concept of flowspaces and how the centralized control feature of OpenFlow provides flexible network slicing. The network topology for this exercise is shown in the following figure, which includes four OpenFlow switches and four hosts. Switches **s1** and **s4** are connected to each other through **s2** via a low bandwidth connection (that is 1 Mbps and defined as `LBW_path` in the following custom topology script in Mininet) and are also connected to each other via **s3** through a high bandwidth (that is 10 Mbps, defined as `HBW_path` in the custom script in Mininet) set of links:

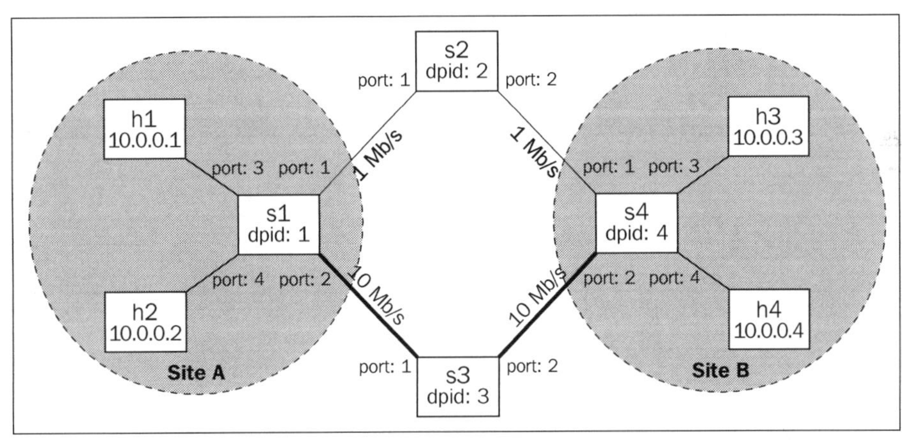

Network topology

This network topology can be constructed using the following Mininet script (assuming that the `flowvisor_topo.py` file is available in the current directory). Mininet installation was presented in *Chapter 2, Implementing OpenFlow Switch* utilized as part of the OpenFlow laboratory in *Chapter 4, Setting Up the Environment*:

```
$ sudo mn --custom flowvisor_topo.py --topo slicingtopo --link tc
--controller remote --mac --arp
```

The customized Python script defines a topology named `slicingtopo`, which then becomes accessible on the command line of Mininet.

```
#!/usr/bin/python
# flowvisor_topo.py
from mininet.topo import Topo
class FVTopo(Topo):
    def __init__(self):
        # Initialize topology
```

```
        Topo.__init__(self)
        # Create template host, switch, and link
        hconfig = {'inNamespace':True}
        LBW_path = {'bw': 1}
        HBW_path = {'bw': 10}
        host_link_config = {}
        # Create switch nodes
        for i in range(4):
            sconfig = {'dpid': "%016x" % (i+1)}
            self.addSwitch('s%d' % (i+1), **sconfig)
        # Create host nodes (h1, h2, h3, h4)
        for i in range(4):
            self.addHost('h%d' % (i+1), **hconfig)
        # Add switch links according to the topology
        self.addLink('s1', 's2', **LBW_path)
        self.addLink('s2', 's4', **LBW_path)
        self.addLink('s1', 's3', **HBW_path)
        self.addLink('s3', 's4', **HBW_path)
        # Add host links
        self.addLink('h1', 's1', **host_link_config)
        self.addLink('h2', 's1', **host_link_config)
        self.addLink('h3', 's4', **host_link_config)
        self.addLink('h4', 's4', **host_link_config)
topos = { 'slicingtopo': ( lambda: FVTopo() ) }
```

After network topology, the next step is to create a configuration for FlowVisor, which will be run in a new console terminal. Assuming that you have already installed FlowVisor on a separate virtual machine, the following command line creates this configuration:

```
$ sudo -u flowvisor fvconfig generate /etc/flowvisor/config.json
```

The fvadmin password can be left blank by just hitting the return (*Enter*) key when prompted. To activate this configuration simply start FlowVisor:

```
$ sudo /etc/init.d/flowvisor start
```

Using the `fvctl` utility, enable the FlowVisor topology controller. The `-f` command line parameter points to a password file. Since no password is set for FlowVisor, the password file could point to `/dev/null`. In order to activate this change, FlowVisor should be restarted:

```
$ fvctl -f /dev/null set-config --enable-topo-ctrl
$ sudo /etc/init.d/flowvisor restart
```

All the OpenFlow switches in the Mininet should have connected to the FlowVisor, when it is started. By getting the configuration of FlowVisor, ensure that it is properly running:

```
$ fvctl -f /dev/null get-config
```

You will see the following FlowVisor configuration (in JSON format) similar to the following screen output if it is running properly:


```
{
 "enable-topo-ctrl": true ,
 "flood-perm": {
  "dpid": "all",
  "slice-name": "fvadmin"
 },
 "flow-stats-cache": 30,
 "flowmod-limit": {
  "fvadmin": {
   "00:00:00:00:00:00:00:01":-1,
   "00:00:00:00:00:00:00:02":-1,
   "00:00:00:00:00:00:00:03":-1,
   "00:00:00:00:00:00:00:04":-1,
   "any": null
  }
 },
 "stats-desc": false,
 "track-flows": false
}
```


FlowVisor configuration in JSON format

Using the following command, list the existing slices and ensure that **fvadmin** (the default slice) is the only one, which is shown in the output of the `fvctl` command:

```
$ fvctl -f /dev/null list-slices
```

Issue the following command to print the existing flow spaces and ensure that there are no existing flowspaces:

```
$ fvctl -f /dev/null list-flowspace
```

Listing the data paths will ensure that all the switches have connected to the FlowVisor. You can check it by executing the following `fvctl` command. Before executing the command, you might have to wait for a few seconds. This will give enough time for the switches (s1, s2, s3, and s4) to connect to FlowVisor:

```
$ fvctl -f /dev/null list-datapaths
```

In the next step, ensure that all the network links are active by running the following command:

```
$ fvctl -f /dev/null list-links
```

The output will print out the DPIDs and source and destination ports, which are connected to each other.

Now, we are ready to slice the network. In this experiment, we will create two physical slices, which are named **Upper** and **Lower** slice, as shown in the following figure:

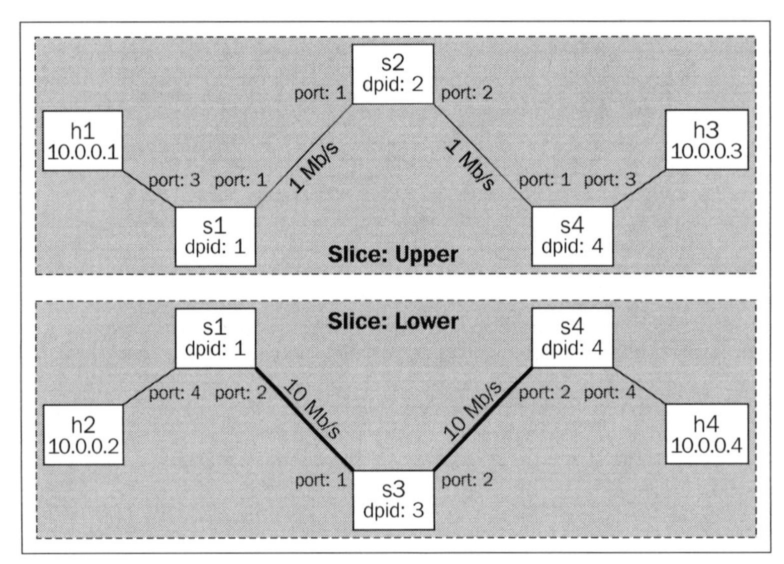

Upper and Lower slices of the experimental network

Each slice can be controlled by a separate controller, which will control all the packet traffic in its own slice. The following command creates a slice named `upper` and connects it to a controller listening on tcp:localhost:10001:

```
$ fvctl -f /dev/null add-slice upper tcp:localhost:10001 admin@upperslice
```

Leave the slice password empty by pressing the return (*Enter*) key when prompted. Similarly, you can create a slice named `lower` and connect it to a controller listening on tcp:localhost:10002. Again, leave the Slice password empty by hitting the return (Enter) key when prompted.

```
$ fvctl -f /dev/null add-slice lower tcp:localhost:10002 admin@lowerslice
```

Now, by executing the `list-slices` command, ensure that the slices were successfully added:

```
$ fvctl -f /dev/null list-slices
```

Besides the default `fvadmin` slice, you should be able to see both the upper and lower slices and all of them should be enabled. In the next step, you will create flowspaces. Flowspaces associate packets of a particular type to specific slices. When a packet matches more than one flowspace, FlowVisor assigns it to the flowspace with the highest priority number. The description of flowspaces comprises a series of comma separated `field=value` assignments. You can learn more about the add-flowspace command by typing:

```
$ fvctl add-flowspace -h
```

Now, we create a flowspace named `dpid1-port1` (with priority value 1) that maps all the traffic on port 1 of switch S1 to the upper slice in the network topology. This can be done by executing the following command:

```
$ fvctl -f /dev/null add-flowspace dpid1-port1 1 1 in_port=1 upper=7
```

Here, we gave the upper slice all permissions: DELEGATE, READ, and WRITE (1 + 4 + 2 = 7). In a similar way, we create a flowspace named `dpid1-port3` that maps all the traffic on port 3 of switch S1 to the upper slice in the network:

```
$ fvctl -f /dev/null add-flowspace dpid1-port3 1 1 in_port=3 upper=7
```

By using the match value of `any`, we can create a flowspace for matching all the traffic at a switch. So, we add switch S2 to the upper slice by running the following command:

```
$ fvctl -f /dev/null add-flowspace dpid2 2 1 any upper=7
```

Now, we create two more flowspaces (`dpid4-port1` and `dpid4-port3`) to add ports 1 and 3 of switch S4 to the upper slice:

```
$ fvctl -f /dev/null add-flowspace dpid4-port1 4 1 in_port=1 upper=7
$ fvctl -f /dev/null add-flowspace dpid4-port3 4 1 in_port=3 upper=7
```

Ensure that these flowspaces are correctly added by running the following command:

```
$ fvctl -f /dev/null list-flowspace
```

You should see all the flowspaces (5 in total) that you just created. Now, we create flowspaces for the lower slice:

```
$ fvctl -f /dev/null add-flowspace dpid1-port2 1 1 in_port=2 lower=7
$ fvctl -f /dev/null add-flowspace dpid1-port4 1 1 in_port=4 lower=7
$ fvctl -f /dev/null add-flowspace dpid3 3 1 any lower=7
$ fvctl -f /dev/null add-flowspace dpid4-port2 4 1 in_port=2 lower=7
$ fvctl -f /dev/null add-flowspace dpid4-port4 4 1 in_port=4 lower=7
```

Again, ensure that the flowspaces are correctly added:

```
$ fvctl -f /dev/null list-flowspace
```

Now, you can launch two OpenFlow controllers on your local host, which are listening on port 10001 and 10002 corresponding to upper and lower slices. You should also write a small Net App that reactively installs routes based on the destination MAC address. After a short delay, both controllers should connect to FlowVisor. Now, you can verify that host h1 can ping h3 but not h2 and h4 (and vice versa).

Run the following command in the Mininet console:

```
mininet> h1 ping -c1 h3
mininet> h1 ping -c1 -W1 h2
mininet> h1 ping -c1 -W1 h4
```

Verify that h2 can ping h4 but not h1 and h3 (and vice versa). Run the following command in the Mininet console:

```
mininet> h2 ping -c1 h4
mininet> h2 ping -c1 -W1 h1
mininet> h2 ping -c1 -W1 h3
```

This concludes a simple network slicing using switch ports. However, by defining other slicing rules and developing other Net Apps, you can provide interesting and innovative services for each slice. For example, you can differentiate traffics and treat them accordingly across the upper and lower network slices. We leave them to you as homework.

Summary

In this chapter we introduced the concept of network virtualization and in particular, the role and functionality of FlowVisor as a tool for network slicing in OpenFlow-based networks. The FlowVisor API and related structures for flow matching and slice actions were presented and a use-case experiment was explained in this chapter. Now you are aware of the tools, which can be used to slice a network and control each slice in an innovative way. In the next chapter, we will look at the role of OpenFlow and SDN in general in cloud computing.

7
OpenFlow in Cloud Computing

This chapter focuses on the role of OpenFlow in cloud computing and in particular the installation and configuration of Neutron will be covered. One of the promises of **SDN** (**Software Defined Networking**) and OpenFlow is the improvement that they can introduce in data centers and a cloud computing infrastructure. Therefore, it is worth covering the usage of OpenFlow (for instance, the Floodlight plugin for OpenStack) in data centers and in particular **OpenStack** as one of the widely used control and management software for cloud computing. A brief introduction to OpenStack and its networking component (which is called Neutron as of this writing) and its overall architecture will be discussed in this chapter. In particular, the installation and the configuration of the Floodlight OpenFlow controller plugin is explained in this chapter. Interested readers are recommended to consider this chapter as a pointer to further details that can be found in the documentation of OpenStack Networking.

OpenStack and Neutron

OpenStack is a cloud computing system software (sometimes referred to as cloud computing OS), which delivers **Infrastructure as a Service** (**IaaS**). Released under Apache License; OpenStack is a free open source software. OpenStack Foundation was established in September 2012 as a non-profit corporate entity, which manages the OpenStack project. It promotes OpenStack and its developer community. OpenStack includes a set of building block projects that control pools of computing nodes (that is processing nodes), storage, and networking resources in a data center. OpenStack provides a dashboard that enables administrators to control and provision the mentioned resources through a web-based (GUI) interface.

OpenStack's modular architecture and its building blocks (and their code names) are shown in the following figure:

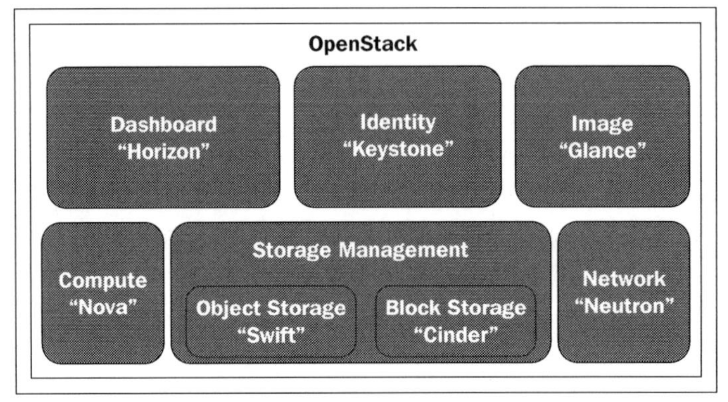

Key components of OpenStack

OpenStack Compute (Nova), which is the main part of an IaaS system, is the cloud computing fabric controller. Nova is written in Python and it utilizes many external libraries such as `SQLAlchemy` (for database access), `Kombu` (for Advanced Message Queuing Protocol communication), and `Eventlet` (for concurrent programming). Nova is able to manage and automate pools of computer resources and can co-operate with widely available virtualization technologies and **High-performance computing** (**HPC**) deployments. It is designed to scale horizontally on commodity computers with no proprietary hardware or software requirements and also to provide the ability to integrate with third party technologies and legacy systems. Xen Server and KVM are the typical choices for hypervisor technology, along with the Linux container technology such as LXC and Hyper-V.

OpenStack utilizes two components for its storage management:

- **Swift**: It is used for object storage management. Swift is also known as OpenStack Object Storage. It is a redundant and scalable storage system. Files and objects are written to multiple disks across multiple servers in the data center. The OpenStack software is responsible for ensuring data integrity and replication across the cluster. By adding new servers, storage clusters simply scale horizontally. If a server or hard drive fails, OpenStack replicates its content to new locations in the cluster from other active nodes. Since OpenStack uses software algorithms to ensure data distribution and data replication across different devices, inexpensive commodity hard disks and servers can be used for storage management.

- **Cinder**: It provides persistent block level storage devices for use with the OpenStack compute instances. Cinder is also known as OpenStack Block Storage. The block storage system is responsible to manage the creation, attachment, and detaching of the block devices to the servers. Block storage is suitable for performance sensitive scenarios such as expandable file systems, database storage, or for providing a server with access to a raw block level storage device. Block storage volumes are fully integrated into Nova (OpenStack compute) and OpenStack's Dashboard. This enables the cloud users to easily manage their own storage requirements. Powerful functionality for backing up data stored on block storage volumes is provided by Snapshot management. Snapshots can be used to create a new block storage volume or simply can be restored.

Horizon is the OpenStack dashboard. It provides a graphical user interface (GUI) for users and administrators to provision, automate, and access to cloud-based resources. Third party products and services, such as monitoring, billing, and additional management tools can be integrated into the Horizon (OpenStack dashboard). Using the native OpenStack API or the Amazon EC2 compatibility API, developers can automate access or build customized tools to manage their resources. OpenStack APIs are compatible with Amazon S3 and Amazon EC2. Therefore, client applications, which are designed and developed for Amazon Web Services can be used with OpenStack.

Keystone (OpenStack Identity component) provides a central directory of users, which are mapped to their accessible OpenStack services. It functions as a common authentication system across the cloud operating system. It can also be integrated with existing backend directory services such as LDAP. Standard username and password credentials, token-based systems, and Amazon Web Services logins are the multiple authentication mechanisms, which are supported by Keystone.

Glance (OpenStack Image Service) provides discovery, registration, and delivery services for server images and disks. Stored server images can be used as a template. It can be also used to store and catalog an infinite number of backups. Glance can store disk and server images in a variety of back-ends, including Swift. A standard **REST** (**Representational State Transfer**) interface is provided by Glance for querying information about disk images and enables clients to stream the disk images to new servers.

Neutron (formerly known as Quantum) is the networking component of OpenStack. It manages networks and IP addresses. Effectively from the Folsom release, Neutron is a supported and core part of the OpenStack platform. Like other components of the cloud operating system, administrators and users can utilize Neutron to increase the utilization of existing resources in a data center. Neutron provides **Networking as a Service** (**NaaS**) between interface devices (for instance vNICs), which are managed by other Openstack services. OpenStack Neutron provides networking models for different user groups or applications. Standard models include VLANS or flat networks for separation of network traffic among different servers. Neutron also manages IP addresses, which can provide dedicated static IPs or DHCP-based IP addressing. Floating IP addressing allows packets' traffic to be dynamically rerouted to any of the computing nodes, which facilitates traffic redirection during VM migration, maintenance, or failure handling. Extensible architecture of Neutron paves the way for additional network services, such as firewalls, intrusion detection systems (IDS), virtual private networks, and load balancing to be deployed and managed. The networking component of OpenStack, provides the OpenStack's users with an API to construct rich networking topologies and configure advanced network policies to construct multitier web application topology. The modular structure of Neutron facilitates the development of innovative plugins, which introduce advanced network capabilities (such as L2-in-L3 tunneling to bypass 4096 VLAN limitation, end-to-end QoS guarantees, and utilization of monitoring protocols such as NetFlow and OpenFlow plugins). Besides, developers can develop advanced network services that integrate into the OpenStack tenant network using plugins. For instance, data-center-interconnect-aaS, IDS-aaS, firewall-aaS, VPN-aaS, and load-balancing-aaS are a few typical advanced services to mention. Using Neutron, users can create their own networks, control traffic, and connect servers and devices to one or more networks, while administrators can take advantage of SDN technology (for instance OpenFlow) to provide high levels of multitenancy and scalability.

OpenStack Networking Architecture

Neutron is able to utilize a set of backends called plugins that support a growing set of networking technologies. These plugins may be distributed separately or as part of the main Neutron release. OpenStack Networking (Neutron) is a virtual network service that provides an efficient API to define the network connectivity and addressing, that is used by devices from other OpenStack services (such as OpenStack Compute). The OpenStack Networking API utilizes virtual network, subnet, and port abstractions to describe networking resources. In the OpenStack networking ecosystem:

- Network is an isolated L2 segment similar to VLAN in the physical networking
- A block of IPv4 or IPv6 addresses and associated configuration states is a subnet
- A connection point for attaching a single device, such as the NIC of a virtual server, to a virtual network is defined as a port. Also, a port describes the network configuration parameters (such as the MAC and IP addresses), which are associated to that port

By creating and configuring networks and subnets, users can configure rich network topologies; and then instructing other OpenStack services such as OpenStack Compute to connect virtual interfaces to ports on these networks. Neutron particularly supports each tenant having multiple private networks, and enables tenants to choose their own IP addressing scheme. The OpenStack Networking service:

- Provides advanced cloud networking scenarios, such as constructing multitiered web applications and enabling applications to be migrated to the cloud without IP addresses' modifications
- Enables cloud administrators to offer flexible and customized network offerings
- Provides API extensions that lets cloud administrators expose additional API capabilities. These new capabilities are typically introduced as an API extension, and gradually will become part of the core OpenStack Networking API

The original OpenStack Compute network implements a very simple model of traffic isolation through IP tables and Linux VLANs. OpenStack Networking introduces the notion of a plugin, which is a backend implementation of the OpenStack Networking API. A plugin can use different technologies to implement the logical API requests. Some OpenStack Networking plugins might use basic Linux VLANs and IP tables, while others might use more advanced technologies, such as L2-in-L3 tunneling or OpenFlow, to provide similar capabilities.

The main module of the OpenStack Networking server is neutron-server, which is a Python daemon that exposes the OpenStack Networking API. It passes user requests to the configured OpenStack Networking plugin for extra processing.

The plugin typically needs a database for persistent storage. If your deployment uses a controller host to run centralized OpenStack Compute components, you can deploy the OpenStack Networking server on that same host. However, OpenStack Networking is completely standalone and can be deployed on its own server. Based on deployment, OpenStack Networking also includes additional agents that might be required:

- The Plugin agent (`neutron-*-agent`), which executes on each hypervisor to configure a local switch. Since some plugins do not actually require an agent, the agent to be run will depend on the selected plugin
- The DHCP agent (`neutron-dhcp-agent`) provides DHCP services to tenant networks
- The L3 agent (`neutron-l3-agent`) provides L3 / NAT forwarding to facilitate external network access for VMs on tenant networks

These agents interact with the core Neutron process through remote procedure call (RPC) or by utilizing the standard OpenStack Networking API. OpenStack Networking relies on the Keystone for the authentication and authorization of all API requests. Nova interacts with OpenStack Networking through standard API calls. During the VM creation process, the Nova communicates with the OpenStack Networking API to plug each virtual network interface card on the VM into a particular network. Horizon integrates with the OpenStack Networking API, and enables tenant users and administrators to create and manage network services through the GUI of the OpenStack dashboard.

There are four distinct physical data center networks in a standard OpenStack networking deployment, as depicted in the following figure (data network connects virtual machines inside the cloud setup and is not shown in the following figure):

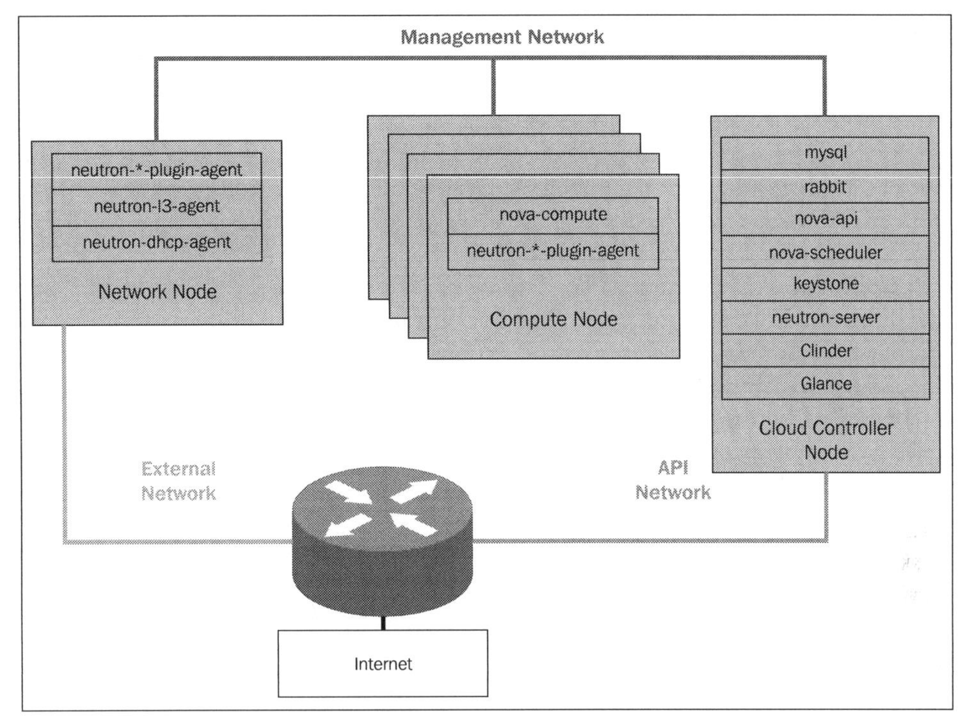

Network connectivity for physical hosts

- **Management network**: It is used for internal communication between OpenStack components. IP addresses assignments on this network should be only reachable within the data center network
- **Data network**: It is used for VM data communication within the cloud setup. Depending on the used networking plugin the IP addressing requirements of this network varies
- **External network**: It is used to provide the Internet access for VMs in some deployments. IP addresses on this network should be visible and reachable by any host on the Internet.
- **API network**: It exposes all OpenStack APIs, including the OpenStack Networking API, to tenants. IP addresses on this network should be reachable by anyone on the Internet

The complete installation and configuration instructions of OpenStack Neutron can be found in the OpenStack networking administration guide. More information can be found here: `http://wiki.openstack.org/wiki/Neutron`.

Neutron plugins

Providing rich cloud networking by enhancing traditional networking solutions is quite challenging. Traditional networking is not scalable to cloud proportions by its design nor to cope with automatic configuration. OpenStack Networking introduces the concept of a plugin, which is a backend implementation of the OpenStack Networking API. In order to implement the logical API requests, a plugin can utilize a variety of technologies. Some plugins might use the Linux IP tables and basic VLANs, while other implementations might use more advanced technologies, such as L2-in-L3 tunneling or OpenFlow. Plugins can have different features for hardware requirements, properties, performance, scale, or operator tools. OpenStack supports a wide spectrum of plugins. Therefore, the cloud administrator is able to consider different options and decide which networking technology fits a particular use case scenario. Among different plugins for Neutron, in this section we will consider the Floodlight controller plugin for OpenStack Neutron.

Utilizing a Neutron plugin, Floodlight can be run as the network backend for OpenStack. Neutron which exposes a NaaS model via a REST API, which is implemented by Floodlight. This solution includes two main components: the Neutron RestProxy plugin that connects Floodlight to Neutron and a VirtualNetworkFilter module in Floodlight that implements the Neutron API. The VirtualNetworkFilter module implements MAC-based layer 2 network isolation in OpenFlow networks and exposes it through a REST API. This module is included in Floodlight by default and does not depend on Neutron or OpenStack to be active and running. The VirtualNetworkFilter can be activated through a configuration file change described later in the chapter. The RestProxy plugin was designed to run as part of OpenStack's Neutron service. Floodlight with the Big Switch Neutron plugin supports OpenStack Grizzly release.

> The Floodlight OpenStack support is enabled by:
>
> The Big Switch Neutron Plugin at the OpenStack Neutron main repo: `http://github.com/openstack/neutron`.
>
> The OpenStack devstack repo stable/grizzly branch: `http://github.com/openstack-dev/devstack/tree/stable/grizzly`.

The following instructions are for setting up Floodlight and OpenStack (Grizzly) on a Ubuntu VM using devstack scripts developed by Big Switch. A virtual machine with Ubuntu Server 12.04.1 or with a later version is required as an installation prerequisite. The outcome of this procedure is a single node OpenStack installation with Floodlight as its Neutron backend. Tenants, virtual networks, and virtual instances can be created by OpenStack Horizon GUI (dashboard).

You will need to execute a Floodlight controller for the OpenStack Neutron networking support to properly function. The floodlight controller can be running on a separate floodlight VM or you can obtain and download the Floodlight source as a compressed ZIP file, unzip it, compile, and run it with the following simple steps on your Ubuntu VM. Make sure you have Internet connectivity before proceeding:

```
$ sudo apt-get update
$ sudo apt-get install zip default-jdk ant
$ wget --no-check-certificate https://github.com/floodlight/floodlight/
archive/master.zip
$ unzip master.zip
$ cd floodlight-master; ant
$ java -jar target/floodlight.jar -cf
src/main/resources/neutron.properties
```

To confirm the VirtualNetworkFilter is successfully activated, enter the following commands on your Ubuntu VM:

```
$ curl 127.0.0.1:8080/networkService/v1.1
{"status":"ok"}
```

Once Floodlight is confirmed running, we are ready to install OpenStack using the install-devstack script. The following are the steps:

1. It configures the OVS switch on the VM to listen to the Floodlight controller.
2. Then, it installs OpenStack and the Big Switch REST proxy plugin on the VM.
3. If you want the OpenStack Grizzly release, use the following commands:

   ```
   $ wget https://github.com/openstack-
   dev/devstack/archive/stable/grizzly.zip
   $ unzip grizzly.zip
   $ cd devstack-stable-grizzly
   ```

4. If you want the OpenStack Folsom release, use the following commands:

   ```
   $ wget
   https://github.com/bigswitch/devstack/archive/floodlight/folsom.
   zip
   $ unzip folsom.zip
   $ cd devstack-floodlight-folsom
   ```

5. Use your favorite editor to create a file named `localrc` and fill in the following details. Remember to replace `<password>` to your chosen password and update `BS_FL_CONTROLLERS_PORT=<floodlight IP address>` with the value `8080`. If you have run Floodlight in the same VM, then use `127.0.0.1` for `<floodlight IP address>;` otherwise, use the IP address of the VM or the host where Floodlight is running on it.

```
disable_service n-net
enable_service q-svc
enable_service q-dhcp
enable_service neutron
enable_service bigswitch_floodlight
Q_PLUGIN=bigswitch_floodlight
Q_USE_NAMESPACE=False
NOVA_USE_NEUTRON_API=v2
SCHEDULER=nova.scheduler.simple.SimpleScheduler
MYSQL_PASSWORD=<password>
RABBIT_PASSWORD=<password>
ADMIN_PASSWORD=<password>
SERVICE_PASSWORD=<password>
SERVICE_TOKEN=tokentoken
DEST=/opt/stack
SCREEN_LOGDIR=$DEST/logs/screen
SYSLOG=True
#IP:Port for the BSN controller
#if more than one, separate with commas
BS_FL_CONTROLLERS_PORT=<ip_address:port>
BS_FL_CONTROLLER_TIMEOUT=10
```

6. Then, enter the following command:

```
$ ./stack.sh
```

Note that OpenStack installation is a long process that cannot be interrupted. Any interruption or loss of network connectivity results in unknown states that cannot be resumed. It is recommended that you take a snapshot using VirtualBox before you begin the installation, such that you can easily power down and restore the original snapshot if indeed the process is interrupted. The script `install-devstack.sh` requires uninterrupted IP connectivity to run. If the installation completes successfully, it will show as the following screenshot:

```
Horizon is now available at http://10.10.2.15  /
Keystone is serving at http://10.10.2.15:5000/v2.0/
Examples on using novaclient command line is in
exercise.sh
The default users are: admin and demo
The password: nova
This is your host ip: 10.10.2.15
stack.sh completed in 103 seconds.
```

> You can verify the installation of OpenStack and Floodlight using the instructions in the following link: `http://docs.projectfloodlight.org/display/floodlightcontroller/Verify+OpenStack+and+Floodlight+Installation`.

Summary

Neutron is an OpenStack project to provide networking as a service (NaaS) among interface devices (known as virtual NICs) managed by other Openstack services (Nova). Starting in the Folsom release of OpenStack, Neutron is a core and supported part of the OpenStack framework. In this chapter, the key building blocks of OpenStack including the Neutron networking component and the backend plugins (specifically the Floodlight plugin) were introduced. The Neutron API, includes support for L2 networking and IP Address Management (IPAM). The API Extensibility platform, including extensions for provider network, which maps Neutron L2 networks to a specific VLAN in the physical data center, network L3 routers support a simple L3 router construct to route between L2 networks. It also provides a gateway to external networks with support for floating IP addresses.
In the final chapter of this book, we provide a selection of key Open Source projects around SDN and OpenFlow.

8
Open Source Resources

SDN and OpenFlow are among the hot topics in networking research and development domain both in industry and academia. There are plenty of active open source projects around SDN and OpenFlow form OpenFlow software-based switches to OpenFlow controllers, orchestration tools, network virtualization tools, simulation and testing tools, and so on. The main idea here is to give a brief and condensed summary of active open source projects around SDN and OpenFlow.
We will cover the following open source projects:

- **Switches**: Open vSwitch, Pantou, Indigo, LINC, XORPlus, OF13SoftSwitch
- **Controllers**: Beacon, Floodlight, Maestro, Trema, FlowER, Ryu
- **Miscellaneous**: FlowVisor, Avior, RouteFlow, OFlops and Cbench, OSCARS, Twister, FortNOX

This chapter gives pointers to the important projects that network engineers can utilize in their operational environment.

Switches

In this section, we will cover the open source projects with focus on OpenFlow soft switching.

Open vSwitch

Hypervisors (for example, Xen, VirtualBox, VMware player) need the ability to bridge traffic between **virtual machines** (**VMs**) and to/from the outside world. Linux bridge as a built-in L2 switch, is and fast a reliable means for that. But Open vSwitch is targeted at multi-server virtualization deployments, for which Linux bridging is not a suitable solution for interconnecting VMs. Multi-server virtualization environments are often characterized by highly dynamic end-points, the maintenance of logical abstractions, and (sometimes) integration with, or offloading to, special purpose switching hardware. Mobility of state, response to network dynamics, maintenance of logical tags, and hardware integration are the key features of Open vSwitch to meet these requirements.

All associated network states with a VM should be easily identified and migrated (if required) between different physical hosts. This may include a traditional soft state (for example an entry in an L2 forwarding table), an L3 forwarding state, ACLs, QoS policy, or monitoring configuration (for instance NetFlow, sFlow), and so on. Open vSwitch has support for both configuring and migrating both slow (configuration) and fast network states between instances.

Virtual environments are often characterized by high rates of change (for example, coming and going of VMs and changes to the logical network environments). Open vSwitch supports a number of features that allow a network control system to respond and adapt as the environment changes. In addition to simple accounting and visibility support such as NetFlow, and sFlow, Open vSwitch supports a network state database (OVSDB) that supports remote triggers. Therefore, a piece of orchestration software can monitor various aspects of the network and respond if/when they change. This can be used to respond to, and track the VM migrations. Open vSwitch also supports OpenFlow as a method of exporting remote access to control traffic.

Distributed virtual switches (for example, VMware, vDS, and Cisco's Nexus 1000V) often maintain a logical context within the network through appending or manipulating tags in network packets. This can be used to uniquely identify a VM, or to hold some other context that is only relevant in the logical domain. Much of the problem of building a distributed virtual switch is to efficiently and correctly manage these tags. Open vSwitch includes multiple mechanisms for specifying and maintaining tagging rules, all of which are accessible to a remote process for orchestration.

The forwarding path in Open vSwitch (that is the in-kernel data path) is designed to offload the packet processing to the hardware chipsets, whether housed in a classic hardware switch chassis or in an end-host NIC. This enables the Open vSwitch to be able to both control a pure software implementation or a hardware switch. The advantage of hardware integration is not only performance within virtualized environments. If physical switches also expose the Open vSwitch control abstractions, both bare-metal and virtualized hosting environments can be managed using the same mechanism for automated network control.

Open vSwitch is a multilayer virtual switch licensed under the Apache license. It is designed to enable massive network automation through programmatic extension, while still supporting standard management interfaces and protocols (for example, NetFlow, sFlow, SPAN, RSPAN, CLI, LACP, 802.1ag). In addition, it is designed to support distribution across multiple physical servers similar to VMware's vNetwork distributed vSwitch or Cisco's Nexus 1000V. (See the following figure):

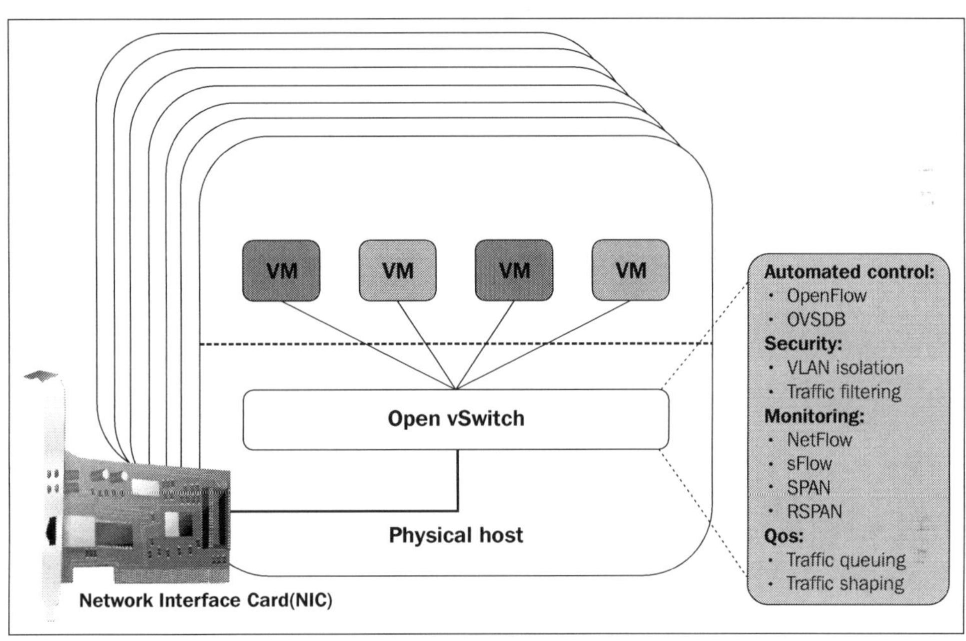

Open vSwitch: Production quality, Multilayer, Open Virtual Switch.

Open vSwitch can operate as both, a soft switch running within the hypervisor, and as the control stack for switching silicon. It has been ported to multiple virtualization platforms and switching chipsets. It is the default switch in XenServer 6.0, the Xen Cloud Platform and also supports Xen, KVM, Proxmox VE, and VirtualBox. It has also been integrated into many virtual management systems including OpenStack, openQRM, OpenNebula and oVirt. The kernel data path is distributed with Linux, and packages are available for Ubuntu, Debian, and Fedora. The Open vSwitch release in development also supports FreeBSD. The bulk of the code is written in platform-independent C and is easily ported to other environments. As of Linux 3.3, Open vSwitch is included as a part of the kernel and packaging for the userspace utilities are available on most popular distributions.

You can find more information about Open vSwitch and download it here: `http://www.openvswitch.org`.

Pantou

Pantou turns a commercial wireless router/access point to an OpenFlow-enabled switch. OpenFlow is implemented as an application on top of OpenWrt. OpenWrt is an operating system primarily used on embedded devices to route network traffic. The main components are the Linux kernel, uClibc, and BusyBox. All components have been optimized for size, to be small enough to fit the limited storage and memory available in home routers. Pantou is based on the BackFire OpenWrt release (Linux 2.6.32). The OpenFlow module is based on the Stanford reference implementation (userspace). To convert your router/access point into an OpenFlow switch, you need to get an appropriate image for your device chipset (currently Broadcom and Atheros), load this image to your device and verify that everything works together. You can also build your own image rather than using one of the provided ones from its source code. It is strongly recommended that you build and load a vanilla OpenWrt tree before adding any OpenFlow-related functionality. The current release of Pantou is based on the BackFire OpenWrt release.

More information about OpenFlow 1.0 for OpenWRT can be found in the following link: `http://www.openflow.org/wk/index.php/OpenFlow_1.0_for_OpenWRT`.

In addition, an OpenFlow 1.3 implementation for OpenWRT can be found in the following link:

`http://github.com/CPqD/openflow-openwrt`.

Indigo

Indigo is an open source OpenFlow implementation that runs on physical switches and uses the hardware features of **application specific integrated circuits** (**ASICs**) of Ethernet switches to run OpenFlow at line rates. It is based on the OpenFlow Reference Implementation from Stanford and currently implements all required features of the OpenFlow 1.0 standard. First Generation implementation of Indio switch is no longer supported. Indigo2 is the basis of Switch Light by Big Switch Networks and the Indigo Virtual Switch. Indigo2 has two components, Indigo2 agent and LoxiGen. The Indigo2 agent represents the core libraries and includes a **hardware abstraction layer** (**HAL**) to make it easy to integrate with the forwarding and port management interfaces of physical or virtual switches, and a configuration abstraction layer to support running OpenFlow in a hybrid mode on a physical switch. LoxiGen is a compiler that generates OpenFlow marshalling/un-marshalling libraries in multiple languages. Currently it supports C (called loci), but Java and Python programming/scripting languages are under development. **Indigo virtual switch** (**IVS**) is a lightweight, high-performance vSwitch built from the ground up to support the OpenFlow protocol. It is designed to enable high-scale network virtualization applications and supports distribution across multiple physical servers using an OpenFlow enabled controller, similar to VMware's vNetwork, Cisco's Nexus, or Open vSwitch.

> More information about the Indigo switch can be found in this URL:
> `http://www.projectfloodlight.org/indigo/`

LINC

LINC is an open source project led by FlowForwarding (`www.flowforwarding.org`) effort and is an Apache 2 license implementation based on OpenFlow 1.2, 1.3.1 and OF-Config 1.1. FlowForwarding is a community promoting free, open source, and commercially friendly Apache 2 license implementation based on OpenFlow and Open Networking Foundation (ONF) specifications. LINC is an ERLANG based switch for Linux.

> An Alpha version of the source code is available at:
> `https://github.com/FlowForwarding`.

XORPlus

With the fast improvement of switching ASICs, the off-the-shelf switch chips (for example Broadcom) have surpassed the performance and density of proprietary designed chips from traditional switch system vendors (for example, Cisco and Brocade). XORPlus fills the gap of an open source switching software to drive high performance ASICs. Pica8 (`www.pica8.org`) XORPlus is a unique open source software, which runs on a data center grade of switch platforms to provide not only high quality of protocol implementation but also a high performance of switching/routing speed. It is a switching software supported by open community. The software supports the most popular L2/L3 protocols the network users would need. XORPlus focuses on solving performance, scalability, and stability issues for data center networks. Among the L2 features of XORPlus, we can mention STP/RSTP/MSTP, LCAP, QoS, 802.1q VLAN, LLDP, and ACL protocols. OSPF/ECMP, RIP, IGMP, IPv6, and PIM-SM are L3 features of XORPlus.

OpenFlow is supported through Open vSwitch (OVS) 1.1 release, which is compliant with OpenFlow 1.0 specification. Most importantly, XORplus enables the community to innovate. Users can develop leading-edge protocols and data traffic management without the limitation of traditional embedded switches. Pica8 XORPlus is independent of the underlying switch chips. It can run on different platforms with high extensibility. The software architecture is designed to allow the protocol stack running on different platforms from the driver and the switching hardware. This allows much more flexible usage models than traditional switches. With the open source software and open platform, users of high performance switches can finally break the lock-in of high-margin proprietary switches.

Pica8 XORPlus URL:
`http://sourceforge.net/projects/xorplus.`

OF13SoftSwitch

OF13SoftSwitch is an OpenFlow 1.3 compatible user-space software switch implementation based on the Ericsson TrafficLab 1.1 SoftSwitch implementation (`http://github.com/TrafficLab/of11softswitch`) with required changes in the forwarding plane to support OpenFlow 1.3. The root code of this project is the reference OpenFlow 1.0 implementation by Stanford University. The following building blocks are included in the OF13SoftSwitch packaging:

- The OpenFlow 1.3 switch implementation: `ofdatapath`
- Secure channel to connect the switch to the OpenFlow controller: `ofprotocol`
- A software library for converting from/to OpenFlow 1.3 wire formant: `oflib`
- A command line utility program (that is `dpctl`) to configure the OF13SoftSwitch from console: `dpctl`

This project is supported by the Ericsson Innovation Center in Brazil and maintained by CPqD in technical collaboration with Ericsson Research. Instructions for installing and downloading the software switch, along with tutorials can be found in the project page in Github. (See the following link). You can try the pre-configured version of OF13SoftSwitch, which includes the OpenFlow 1.3 Software Switch, a compatible version of NOX controller, the plugin to the Wireshark dissector and OpenFlow test suite (OF-test).

[For more information visit the OpenFlow 1.3 softswitch project, this is located at: `http://cpqd.github.io/ofsoftswitch13/`]

Controllers

In *Chapter 4, Setting Up the Environment*, we covered POX, and OpenDaylight OpenFlow controllers. In this section we provide a list of other open source OpenFlow controller alternatives.

Beacon

Beacon is a fast, cross-platform, modular, Java-based controller that supports both event-based and threaded operation. Beacon has been in development since early 2010, and has been used in several research projects, networking classes, and trial deployments. It is written in Java and runs on many platforms, from high end multi-core Linux servers to Android phones. Beacon is licensed under a combination of the GPL v2 license and the Stanford University FOSS License Exception v1.0. Code bundles in Beacon can be started/stopped/refreshed/installed at runtime, without interrupting other non-dependent bundles. For example, you can replace your running `Learning Switch` Net App without disconnecting switches.

[You can find more information about this controller here: `https://openflow.stanford.edu/display/Beacon/Home`]

Floodlight

The Floodlight Open SDN Controller is an enterprise-class, Apache-licensed, Java-based OpenFlow Controller. It is supported by a community of developers including a number of engineers from Big Switch Networks. Floodlight is written in Java and thus runs within a JVM. The source code repository is available on Github. The easiest way to get started with Floodlight is to download the Floodlight VM appliance. In addition of being an OpenFlow controller, Floodlight is also a collection of applications built on top of the Floodlight Controller. The controller realizes a set of common functionalities to control and inquire an OpenFlow network, while applications on top of the Floodlight controller realizes different features to solve different user requirements over the network. The architecture of Floodlight is shown in the following figure.

The relationship among the Floodlight Controller, the applications built as Java modules compiled with Floodlight, and the network applications built over the Floodlight REST API are shown in this figure

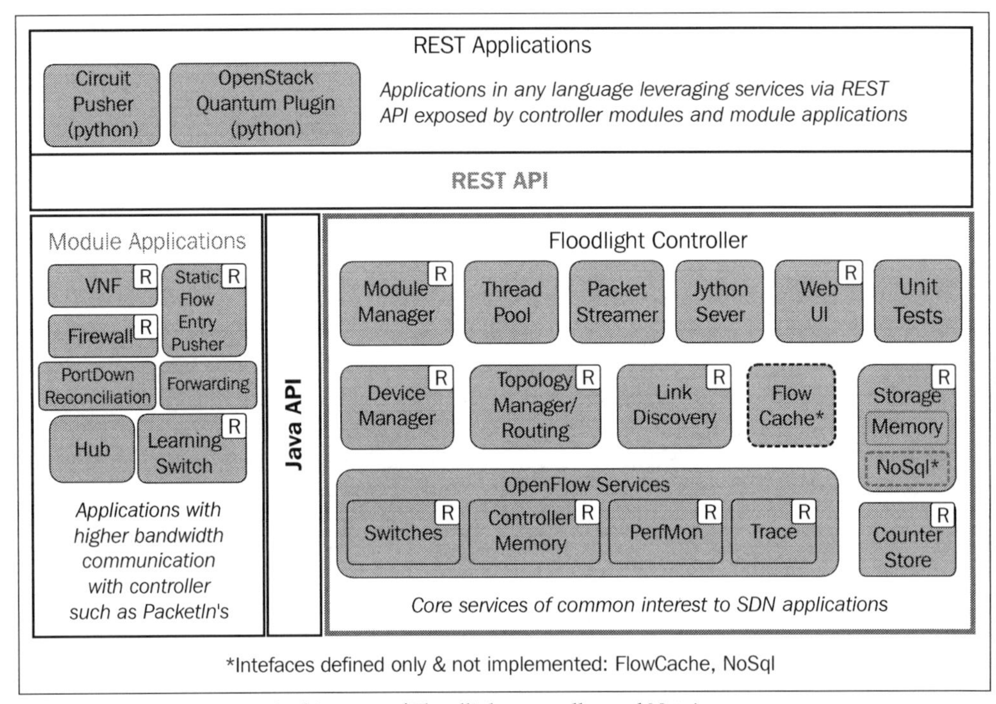

Architecture of Floodlight controller and Net Apps

When you start Floodlight controller, a set of Java module applications, which are loaded in the Floodlight properties file (for example, learning switch, hub, firewall, and static flow entry pusher) start running too. The REST APIs exposed by all running modules are available via the specified REST port (8080 by default). Other Net Apps (for example, OpenStack quantum plug-in, or circuit pusher) can utilize this REST API to retrieve information and invoke services by sending http REST commands to the controller REST port.

You can find more information about Floodlight in the following URL:
`http://www.projectfloodlight.org/floodlight/`

Maestro

Maestro is a network operating system for orchestrating network control applications. Maestro provides interfaces for implementing modular network control applications to access and modify the state of the network, and coordinate their interactions via multiple protocols including OpenFlow. Although it can be considered as an OpenFlow controller, Maestro is not limited to OpenFlow networks. The programming framework of Maestro provides interfaces for:

- Introducing new customized control functions by adding modularized control components.
- Maintaining the network state on behalf of the control components.
- Composing control components by specifying the execution sequencing and the shared network state of the components.

Maestro is developed in Java (both the platform and the components), which makes it highly portable to various operating systems and architectures. It also takes full advantage of multi-core processors using multi-threading techniques. Maestro is licensed under the GNU Lesser General Public License version 2.1.

For more details about downloading, using, and programming Maestro, please visit: `http://code.google.com/p/maestro-platform/`

Trema

Trema is an OpenFlow controller framework that includes everything needed to create OpenFlow controllers in Ruby and C. Trema source package includes basic libraries and functional modules that work as an interface to OpenFlow switches. Several sample applications developed on top of Trema are also provided, so you can run them as a sample of the OpenFlow controllers. Additionally, a simple but powerful framework that emulates an OpenFlow-based network and end-hosts is provided for testing your own controllers. A Wireshark plug-in to diagnose internal data-flows among functional modules is provided as a debugging tool. Currently, Trema supports GNU/Linux only and it has been tested on the following platforms:

- Ubuntu 13.04, 12.10, 12.04, 11.10, and 10.04 (i386/amd64, Desktop Edition)
- Debian GNU/Linux 7.0 and 6.0 (i386/amd64)
- Fedora 16 (i386/x86_64)
- Ruby 1.8.7
- RubyGems 1.3.6 or higher

It may also run on other GNU/Linux distributions but is not tested and not supported as of this writing.

You can find more information about Trema here: `github.com/trema`.

FlowER

FlowER is an open-source Erlang based OpenFlow controller. Its purpose is to provide a simplified platform for writing network control software in Erlang. It is currently under development but Travelping (`www.travelping.com`), creator of FlowER, is already using it in its commercial products. FlowER is built for the deployment model that packages each Erlang application either as an RPM or DEB package.

You can find more information about FlowER here: `http://github.com/travelping/flower`

Ryu

Ryu is a component-based SDN framework that integrates with OpenStack and supports OpenFlow. It provides a logically centralized controller and a well-defined API that make it easy for operators to create new network management and control applications. Ryu supports various protocols for managing network devices, such as OpenFlow (1.0, 1.2, 1.3 and Nicira extensions), Netconf, OF-config, and so on. The goal of Ryu is to develop an operating system for SDN that has high quality enough for use in a large production environment. All of the code is freely available under the Apache 2.0 license.

Utilizing Ryu, operators can create tens of thousands of isolated virtual networks without using VLAN. You can create and manage virtual networks, which will be propagated to OpenStack and Ryu plug-in. Ryu, in turn, configures Open vSwitches properly. The pre-configured Ryu VM image file enables the operators to easily set up a multi-node OpenStack environment. Ryu is implemented in Python and its development is truly open.

You can find more information about Ryu here: `http://osrg.github.io/ryu/`.

Miscellaneous

In addition to the soft switches and controllers, there are many other open source projects around OpenFlow and SDN. In this section we give pointers to some of the important open source projects.

FlowVisor

A software-defined network can have some level of logical decentralization, with multiple logical controllers. An interesting type of proxy controller, called FlowVisor, can be utilized to add a level of network virtualization to OpenFlow networks and allow multiple controllers to simultaneously control overlapping sets of physical switches. Initially developed to allow experimental research to be conducted on deployed networks alongside production traffic. It also facilitates and demonstrates the ease of deploying new services in SDN environments. FlowVisor is a special purpose OpenFlow controller that acts as a transparent proxy between OpenFlow switches and multiple OpenFlow controllers as depicted in the following figure:

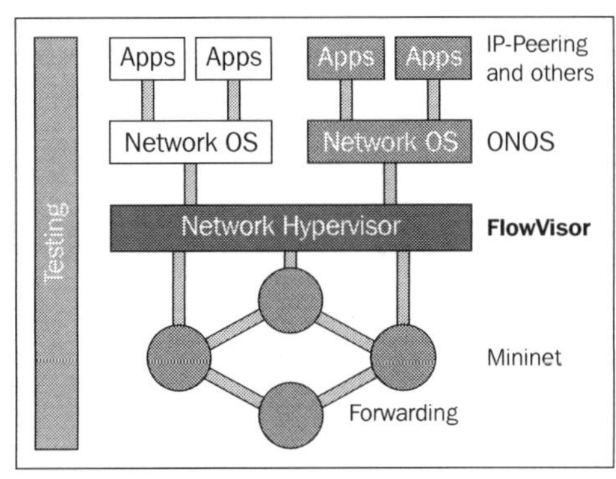

FlowVisor as a network slicer.

FlowVisor creates rich slices of network resources and delegates control of each slice to a different controller and also promoting isolation between slices. FlowVisor, originally developed at Stanford University, has been widely used in experimental Research & Education networks to support slicing where multiple experimenters get their own isolated slice of the infrastructure and control it using their own network OS and a set of control and management applications. FlowVisor enables you to conduct network research in real production environments and using real network traffic. As an open source proxy controller, you can customize the code to adapt to your needs, with a configuration and monitoring interface in `JSON` for users, and a Java programming language for developers, everyone has the ability to customize by opt-in to different services. You can freely and quickly experiment with SDN, with all the foundational SDN functions that enable you to learn about network virtualization and test new methods for deploying services rapidly. Since it is based on open standards that can run on a multi-vendor infrastructure, it supports multiple vendors (for example, NEC, HP, Pronto, OVS, and so on), as well as multiple guest network OSes (that is OpenFlow controllers).

> We introduced FlowVisor in *Chapter 6, How to get a Network Slice*, as part of our discussion about network virtualization; you can find more information about FlowVisor and download it from here: `http://onlab.us/flowvisor.html`.

Avior

Avior is an application built outside of Floodlight that gives network administrators a graphical user interface to support their needs. Avior eliminates dependency on using python scripts or viewing the REST API in order to monitor or manipulate the network. Avior provides an overview of the controller, switch, device, and it includes a flow manager. The controller overview provides information about the controller including the hostname, the JVM memory bloat, whether the controller is providing JSON data, and currently loaded modules. The switch overview provides information about ports and their associated traffic counters and flow table entries. Both dynamic and static flows are displayed with the priority, match, action, packets, bytes, duration, and timeout details. The device overview displays information about the MAC address, the IP address, the attached switch DPID, the attached switch port, and the time it was last seen in the network. The flow manager provides an overview and detailed information of the static flows for each switch. Here you can also manage (add or delete) flow entries. In summary Avior supports a number of useful features as follows:

- Static flow entry pusher interface: Add, modify, and delete flows easily
- Useful error checking and flow verification

- Detailed controller, switch, device, port, and flow statistics that update in real time
- Easy to use Logical patch panel

[Avior is developed for the Marist OpenFlow Research project (`openflow.marist.edu`). You can download it and find more information about Avior here: `http://github.com/Sovietaced/Avior`.]

RouteFlow

RouteFlow is an open source project to provide virtualized IP routing over OpenFlow capable hardware. It is composed by an OpenFlow controller application, an independent server, and a virtual network environment that reproduces the connectivity of a physical infrastructure and runs IP routing engines. The routing engines generate the **forwarding information base** (**FIB**) into the Linux IP tables, according to the routing protocols configured (for example, OSPF, BGP). RouteFlow combines the flexibility of open-source Linux-based routing stacks (for example Quagga, XORP) with the line-rate performance of OpenFlow devices. RouteFlow allows for a migration path to the SDN via a controller-centric hybrid IP networking in addition to deployable innovation around IP routing and the different flavors of network virtualization. The main components of the RouteFlow solution are:

- **RouteFlow Client** (**RF-Client**)
- **RouteFlow Server**
- **RouteFlow Proxy** (**RF-Proxy**)

RF-Proxy which was formerly known as the **RF-Controller** (**RF-C**) application (see the following figure). The main goal of RouteFlow is to develop an open source framework for virtual IP routing solutions over a commodity hardware, which implements the OpenFlow API. RouteFlow aims at a commodity routing architecture that combines the line-rate performance of commercial hardware with the flexibility of open source routing stacks (remotely) running on general purpose computers.

The migration path from legacy IP deployments to purely SDN/OpenFlow networks, open source framework to support the different flavors of network virtualization (for example, logical routers, router aggregation/multiplexing), IP Routing-as-a-Service models of networking and simplified intra and inter-domain routing interoperable with legacy networking devices, are key outcomes of design space of RouteFlow routing solutions.

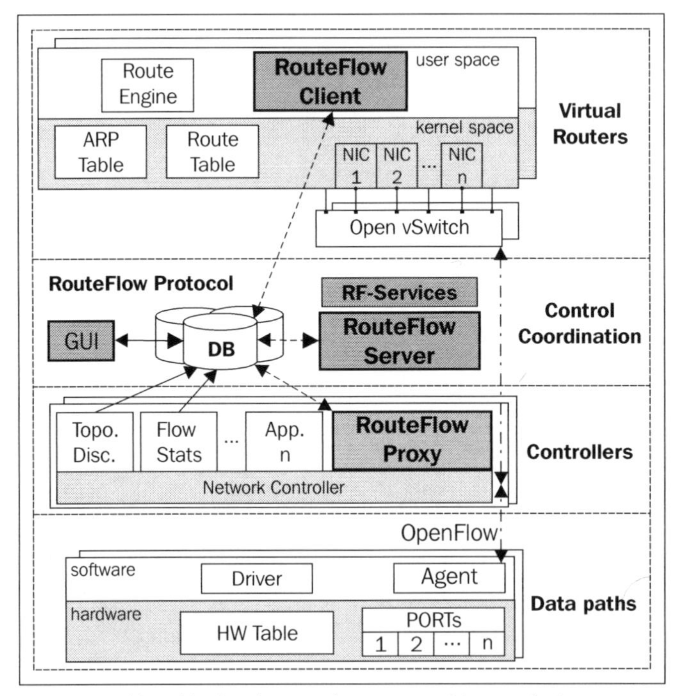

Building blocks of RouteFlow in an architectural view

You can find more information about RouteFlow here: `http://sites.google.com/site/routeflow/home`.

OFlops and Cbench

OFlops is a standalone controller that benchmarks various aspects of an OpenFlow switch. OFlops implements a modular framework for adding and running implementation-agnostic tests to quantify a switch's performance. OFlops sets up a single control channel with the switch and uses multiple network ports to generate traffic on the data plane (OpenFlow switch). Besides, OFlops supports an SNMP protocol in order to read various MIB counters such as CPU utilization, packet counters, and so on. OFlops has two building blocks:

- The executable program, which implements the core functionality of the platform
- A set of dynamically loaded libraries that implement the required functionality for a specific performance evaluation

These components communicate with each other using a rich set of event-driven APIs. Each dynamic test can implement a subset of the provided event handler and adjust the behavior of OFlops. OFlops performs multi-level high precision measurements in order to benchmark the performance of the switch. It utilizes multi-threading parallelism. Cbench is a program for testing OpenFlow controllers by generating packet-in events for new flows. Cbench emulates a bunch of switches, which connect to a controller, sends packet-in messages, and waits for flow-mods to get pushed down.

You can find more information about OFlops and Cbench here: `http://www.openflow.org/wk/index.php/Oflops`.

OSCARS

Energy Services Network (**ESnet**) **On-Demand Secure Circuits and Advance Reservation System** (**OSCARS**) provides multi-domain, high-bandwidth virtual circuits that guarantee end-to-end network data transfer performance. OSCARS software works as both a framework for research innovation and as a reliable production level service for ESnet users. While ESnet offers a menu of service components to novice users, ESnet is exploring an integrated services framework to assist experienced users to configure highly modular atomic services as desired, and for network researchers to customize according to experimental parameters.

You can find more information here: `http://www.es.net/services/virtual-circuits-oscars`.

Twister

Luxoft Twister is a test automation framework designed to manage and drive test cases written in shell scripting languages. Twister supports TCL, Python, and Perl. Twister offers an intuitive, web-based user interface for configuration, control, and reporting with remote access availability. This makes it easy to build the testing suite, execute it, and accurately monitor the result logs.

For more information see: `http://github.com/Luxoft/Twister`.

FortNOX

FortNOX is an extension to the open-source NOX OpenFlow controller. FortNOX automatically checks whether the new flow rules violate security policies. FortNOX can detect rule contradictions, even in the presence of dynamic flow tunneling using set action rules.

For more information please refer to:
`www.openflowsec.org/OpenFlow_Security/Home.html`.

Nettle

Nettle allows networks of OpenFlow switches to be controlled using a high-level, declarative and expressive language. It is implemented on a Haskell library that supports the OpenFlow protocol and provides an OpenFlow server.

You can find more information about Nettle here:
`haskell.cs.yale.edu/nettle`.

Frenetic

Frenetic is a domain-specific language for programming OpenFlow networks, embedded in Python.

For more information go to:
`www.frenetic-lang.org`.

OESS

NDDI OESS is an application to configure and control OpenFlow Enabled switches through a very simple and user-friendly User Interface. OESS provides sub-second circuit provisioning, automatic failover, per-interface permissions, and automatic per-VLAN statistics.

For more information refer to: `http://code.google.com/p/nddi/`.

Summary

Software-defined networking and OpenFlow are among the very hot topics both in academia and industry. There are a lot of commercial and open source developments around OpenFlow and SDN in general. In this chapter, we provided an overview of important open source projects around SDN/OpenFlow. Open vSwitch, Pantou, Indigo, LINC, XORPlus, and OF13SoftSwitch were among the important and active open source projects around the SDN/OpenFlow switching. Beacon, Floodlight, Maestro, Trema, FlowER, and Ryu were additional SDN/OpenFlow controllers that we covered in this chapter. Besides, we also briefly mentioned other important active projects like FlowVisor, Avior, RouteFlow, OFLops and Cbench, OSCARS, Twister, FortNOX, Nettle, Frenetic, and OESS.

Index

Symbols

A

B

C

D

E

F

G

H

I

P

R

S

T

V

X

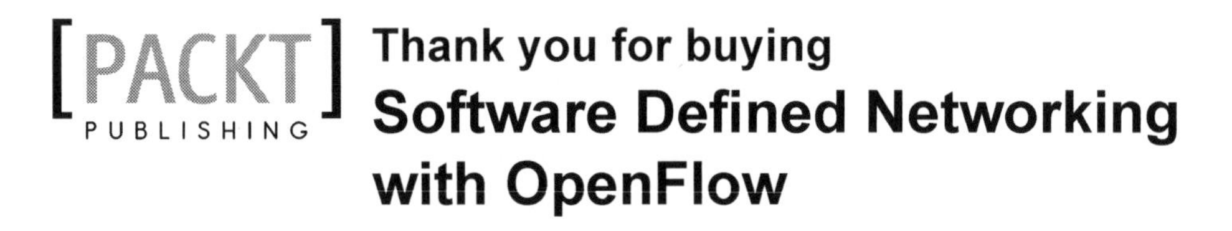

About Packt Publishing

Packt, pronounced 'packed', published its first book "*Mastering phpMyAdmin for Effective MySQL Management*" in April 2004 and subsequently continued to specialize in publishing highly focused books on specific technologies and solutions.

Our books and publications share the experiences of your fellow IT professionals in adapting and customizing today's systems, applications, and frameworks. Our solution based books give you the knowledge and power to customize the software and technologies you're using to get the job done. Packt books are more specific and less general than the IT books you have seen in the past. Our unique business model allows us to bring you more focused information, giving you more of what you need to know, and less of what you don't.

Packt is a modern, yet unique publishing company, which focuses on producing quality, cutting-edge books for communities of developers, administrators, and newbies alike. For more information, please visit our website: `www.packtpub.com`.

Writing for Packt

We welcome all inquiries from people who are interested in authoring. Book proposals should be sent to `author@packtpub.com`. If your book idea is still at an early stage and you would like to discuss it first before writing a formal book proposal, contact us; one of our commissioning editors will get in touch with you.

We're not just looking for published authors; if you have strong technical skills but no writing experience, our experienced editors can help you develop a writing career, or simply get some additional reward for your expertise.

Raspberry Pi Networking Cookbook

ISBN: 978-1-84969-460-5 Paperback: 204 pages

A practical collection of awesome Raspberry Pi recipes that help you learn about the Internet of Things

1. Learn how to install, administer, and maintain your Raspberry Pi
2. Create a network fileserver for sharing documents, music, and videos
3. Host a web portal, collaboration wiki, or even your own wireless access point
4. Connect to your desktop remotely, with minimum hassle

Network Backup with Bacula How-To

ISBN: 978-1-84951-984-7 Paperback: 56 pages

Create an autonomous backup solution for your computer network using practical, hands-on recipes

1. Learn something new in an Instant! A short, fast, focused guide delivering immediate results.
2. Set up Bacula infrastructure.
3. Back up data and directories
4. Work with multiple-storage systems

Please check **www.PacktPub.com** for information on our titles

Network Analysis using Wireshark Cookbook

ISBN: 978-1-84951-764-5 Paperback: 385 pages

110 receipes to analyze and troubleshoot network problems using Wireshark

1. Place Wireshark in your network and configure it for effective network analysis

2. Configure capture and display filters to get the required data

3. Use Wireshark's powerful statistical tools to analyze your network and its expert system to pinpoint network problems

---

SolarWinds Orion Network Performance Monitor

ISBN: 978-1-84968-848-2 Paperback: 336 pages

An essential guide for installing, implementing, and calibrating SolarWinds Orion NPM

1. Master wireless monitoring and the control of wireless access points

2. Learn how to respond quickly and efficiently to network issues with SolarWinds Orion NPM

3. Build impressive reports to effectively visualize issues, solutions, and the overall health of your network

Please check **www.PacktPub.com** for information on our titles

Made in the USA
Middletown, DE
08 October 2016